Thinking Critically: Performance-Enhancing Drugs

Other titles in the *Thinking Critically* series include:

Thinking Critically: Cell Phones
Thinking Critically: Gun Control
Thinking Critically: Social Networking

Thinking Critically: Performance-Enhancing Drugs

Stephen Currie

San Diego, CA

Printed in the United States

For more information, contact:
ReferencePoint Press, Inc.
PO Box 27779
San Diego, CA 92198
www.ReferencePointPress.com

Picture Credits:
All charts and graphs by Maury Aaseng

LIBRARY OF CONGRESS CATALOGING-IN-PUBLICATION DATA

Name: Currie, Stephen, 1960– author.
Title: Thinking Critically: Performance-Enhancing Drugs/by Stephen Currie.
Description: San Diego, CA: ReferencePoint Press, Inc., 2018. | Series: Thinking Critically | Audience: Grade 9 to 12. | Includes bibliographical references and index.
Identifiers: LCCN 2017047106 (print) | LCCN 2017047263 (ebook) | ISBN 9781682823408 (eBook) | ISBN 9781682823392 (hardback)
Subjects: LCSH: Athletes—Drug use. | Doping in sports.
Classification: LCC RC1230 (ebook) | LCC RC1230 .C87 2018 (print) | DDC 362.29088/796—dc23
LC record available at https://lccn.loc.gov/2017047106

Contents

Foreword

"Literacy is the most basic currency of the knowledge economy we're living in today." Barack Obama (at the time a senator from Illinois) spoke these words during a 2005 speech before the American Library Association. One question raised by this statement is: What does it mean to be a literate person in the twenty-first century?

E.D. Hirsch Jr., author of *Cultural Literacy: What Every American Needs to Know*, answers the question this way: "To be culturally literate is to possess the basic information needed to thrive in the modern world. The breadth of the information is great, extending over the major domains of human activity from sports to science."

But literacy in the twenty-first century goes beyond the accumulation of knowledge gained through study and experience and expanded over time. Now more than ever literacy requires the ability to sift through and evaluate vast amounts of information and, as the authors of the Common Core State Standards state, to "demonstrate the cogent reasoning and use of evidence that is essential to both private deliberation and responsible citizenship in a democratic republic."

The *Thinking Critically* series challenges students to become discerning readers, to think independently, and to engage and develop their skills as critical thinkers. Through a narrative-driven, pro/con format, the series introduces students to the complex issues that dominate public discourse—topics such as gun control and violence, social networking, and medical marijuana. Each chapter revolves around a single, pointed question such as Can Stronger Gun Control Measures Prevent Mass Shootings?, or Does Social Networking Benefit Society?, or Should Medical Marijuana Be Legalized? This inquiry-based approach introduces student researchers to core issues and concerns on a given topic. Each chapter includes one part that argues the affirmative and one part that argues the negative—all written by a single author. With the single-author format the predominant arguments for and against an issue can be synthesized into clear, accessible discussions supported by details and evidence including relevant facts, direct quotes, current examples, and statistical illustrations. All volumes include focus questions to guide students as they read each pro/con discussion, a list of key facts, and an annotated list of related organizations and websites for conducting further research.

The authors of the Common Core State Standards have set out the particular qualities that a literate person in the twenty-first century must have. These include the ability to think independently, establish a base of knowledge across a wide range of subjects, engage in open-minded but discerning reading and listening, know how to use and evaluate evidence, and appreciate and understand diverse perspectives. The new *Thinking Critically* series supports these goals by providing a solid introduction to the study of pro/con issues.

Overview

Performance-Enhancing Drugs

The greatest sprinter in the history of the modern Olympic Games is almost certainly Usain Bolt. Born in Jamaica in 1986, Bolt specialized in the 100-meter and 200-meter track events. Bolt won each of these races in the Olympic Games in 2008 and repeated the achievement in the Olympics of 2012 and 2016. No one before had won both events in two consecutive Olympics, let alone three. In addition, Bolt headed up the Jamaican relay team for the 400-meter relay in each of the three Olympics, with his team finishing first in all three races. Between the individual events and the relays, Bolt won an astonishing nine gold medals in Olympic competition—ranking him among the most accomplished Olympic athletes in any sport.

But even though Bolt or his team finished first in nine races, he does not have nine medals. Like most of the rest of the sports world, Olympic authorities bar athletes from using a variety of substances believed to artificially improve performance. Following each event, the blood and urine of medal winners are tested for these substances, known collectively as performance-enhancing drugs, or PEDs. Moreover, since drug tests have become more sensitive over the years, Olympic officials save samples and retest them years later in an attempt to identify every PED-taking competitor. In January 2017 Olympic officials announced that a retest of samples provided by Nesta Carter, one of Bolt's teammates in the 2008 relay event, revealed that Carter had used a forbidden drug known as methylhexanamine during the competition. As a penalty, Olympic authorities stripped Carter and his teammates of the 2008 gold medal for the 100-meter relay and wrote the Jamaicans out of the record books. Officially, Bolt has won only eight gold medals in his illustrious career, not nine.

Bolt's story is one of dozens revealing the importance—and controversies—surrounding the use of PEDs in sports. The list of sports figures penalized for PED use includes some of the world's best-known athletes, among them cyclist Lance Armstrong, tennis player Maria Sharapova, soccer player Diego Maradona, and many others. In addition, some well-known sporting events and records have been especially affected by PED use. In the 2005 Tour de France long-distance bicycle race, for example, every one of the first seven finishers tested positive for PEDs at some point later in his career. And PED use has sparked intense debates within the world of sports, with athletes, officials, and ordinary fans arguing about the legitimacy of PED use, the level of penalties that should be applied, and much more. To a large degree, to follow sports today is to have an opinion about PED use.

Hundreds of Performance-Enhancing Substances

It has been widely known for generations that certain drugs have the effect of increasing muscle mass, raising the level of activity in the body's nervous system, or making it easier for an athlete to bounce back after a punishing workout or competition. Indeed, athletes of the early twentieth century often used drugs to improve their speed, strength, or focus. American runner Thomas Hicks, an entrant in the 1904 Olympic marathon, took small amounts of a poison called strychnine to provide him with extra energy. He went on to win the gold medal. Hicks and his contemporaries also used alcohol, caffeine, and cocaine. Cocaine, which was still legal, was particularly popular among early world-class athletes, writes scientist Thomas H. Murray, because it "staved off the sense of fatigue and hunger brought on by prolonged exertion."[1]

Over time, these drugs became more specialized and more sophisticated. The intersection of science and sport has led to the discovery

Most-Used PEDs in Sports

The drugs in this table are among those most commonly taken by athletes who are hoping to improve their performance. These are also the drugs most commonly tested for at sporting events such as the Olympics. Different drugs affect the body in different ways, so an athlete looking to build strength might use a different category of drug from an athlete hoping to increase alertness or oxygen capacity. At the same time, each type of drug carries its own set of risks for the user. Taking PEDs can have a negative impact on the health of an athlete, both at the time the drug is taken and afterward.

Drug	Effects
Anabolic steroid	• Increases strength and muscle mass • Increases production of testosterone • Reduces muscle damage to help recover from injury faster
Androstenedione	• Helps athletes recover quickly from injury • Allows athletes to train harder
Human growth hormone (HGH)	• Enhances muscle mass and performance
Erythropoietin	• Improves movement of oxygen to the muscles
Creatine*	• Enables muscles to produce more energy
Stimulants	• Improve endurance, reduce fatigue, suppress appetite, increase aggressiveness
Diuretics	• Dilute the urine to help athletes pass drug tests

*Food supplement

Source: Joseph Njoroge, "These Are the Most Used Performance Enhancing Drugs in Sports," Blasting News, June 6, 2017. http://us.blastingnews.com.

or development of hundreds of substances that can improve an athlete's strength, speed, or coordination. The anabolic steroid, one of the best-known PEDs, was developed in the 1950s to help build muscle mass in chronically ill patients. It turned out to improve the strength of world-class athletes as well and was soon adopted by competitors around the globe. Human growth hormone (HGH), which assists the growth process in healthy children, is another example. Giving extra doses of this hormone increases muscle mass and can encourage growth in unusually short children whose bodies do not make sufficient hormones on their own. However, athletes eager for an edge quickly learned that dosing themselves with HGH might boost their strength and size too.

Other substances improve athletic performance in different ways. Erythropoietin (EPO), for example, increases the number of red blood cells in the body. Like many other PEDs, EPO was originally developed to address medical issues. Among other tasks, red blood cells circulate oxygen throughout the body, and medical researchers found EPO helpful in treating patients with low levels of red blood cells. Athletes and trainers, however, soon discovered that EPO injections would increase red blood cells in healthy people as well, thus allowing them to increase the amount of oxygen in their system. And methylhexanamine, the substance that cost Bolt one of his gold medals, is an artificially developed stimulant that can elevate heart rate, improve attention, and increase wakefulness. Today athletes have an enormous variety of drugs like these at their disposal.

Number of Users

Just how many athletes take PEDs is impossible to say. The only official measurement is based on the number of athletes who fail drug tests, as Carter did, and that figure is small. In the National Basketball Association, for example, just seven players failed tests for PEDs between 2006 and 2017. Similarly, only three athletes were stripped of their medals during or immediately after the 2016 Summer Olympics, though the numbers were higher in the previous two competitions. However, most experts doubt that the number of failed drug tests reflects the number of athletes who are doping. Success in sports translates to money and fame, so athletes who dope have a strong incentive not to be found out. They use drugs that are hard to identify in testing or buy PEDs that have only recently been created in the lab. They know that drug testing may miss small quantities of some substances and that tests cannot identify some new drugs at all. Lance Armstrong, for example, finished first in seven consecutive Tour de France competitions in the early 2000s but never failed a drug test during that time. He later admitted to doping during that period.

To get a better idea of the numbers of PED users, some investigators have carried out unofficial drug tests in which athletes are not penalized for a positive result. In one of the most respected studies of this kind, British researchers tested elite track and field athletes in 2011 and found that one-third to one-half of the competitors tested for the study had most likely used banned substances. Estimates vary by sport and even by country. Gymnasts and golfers, for example, are believed to use PEDs less than cyclists or weight lifters, though no one knows for sure. Recent reports from the World Anti-Doping Agency (WADA), similarly, indicated that Russian Olympic team officials were engaged in a program of giving PEDs to hundreds of their best athletes. In 2016 WADA accused Russia of a "systematic and centralized cover-up"[2] of its activities.

Concern and Passion

The reason for concern over PEDs is twofold. One is health. Many PEDs are associated with significant health risks, from the development of acne to liver conditions, heart problems, and cancer. Also of concern is the widespread belief that the use of PEDs amounts to cheating. Banned substances, the argument goes, unfairly boost the skills of users by artificially improving athletes' reaction times, stamina, or muscle mass. Instead of putting in the time and effort needed to become a world-class athlete, PED opponents say, athletes need only pop a pill or give themselves an injection. In this view, drugs allow mediocre athletes to make a living at their chosen sport and catapult good players into the ranks of the best ever. "They wouldn't have been great players without drugs,"[3] argues National Baseball Hall of Fame slugger Frank Thomas, referring to many of baseball's star players of the 1990s and early 2000s.

What can—and should—be done about PEDs has been a hotly debated issue since at least the 1970s, when coaches and trainers of the enormously successful East German women's swimming team were accused (accurately, as it turned out) of giving PEDs to their athletes. Events since then have done nothing to dampen the debate. That should be no surprise, as the stakes are high. Athletes who dope may raise their chances of winning—but if they are caught, they risk humiliation and disgrace. The possibility that an athlete may be doping stirs up strong passions on both sides. As long as drug use is a part of sports, the controversies surrounding PED use will continue.

Chapter One

Should PED Use by Athletes Be Acceptable?

PED Use by Athletes Should Be Acceptable

- Drug testing is expensive, demeaning, and ineffective.
- Drug testing generally fails to detect drug cheats.
- The rules regarding what is (and is not) banned are often arbitrary.
- Adults should be allowed to make their own decisions about what goes into their bodies.

PED Use by Athletes Should Not Be Allowed

- PEDs represent a major health risk to athletes.
- The use of drugs is unethical and drastically changes the definition of sport.
- Drug policy should reward people who work hard.
- Allowing drugs opens the door to even bigger changes in sports.

PED Use by Athletes Should Be Acceptable

"Why not give up the pretense that there's any feasible way to police doping in sports and allow professional athletes to ingest and inject their favorite drugs and pursue any training regimen they wish?"

—Lorie Eber, nutritionist and wellness coach

Lorie Eber, "Let's Stop the Pretense of Drug Testing of Professional Athletes," *Huffington Post*, April 24, 2013. www.huffingtonpost.com.

Consider these questions as you read:

1. Which of the arguments presented in this section do you find the most compelling—and why?
2. How would cheaper or more reliable drug testing change the argument that PED use by athletes should be acceptable?
3. To what extent do you agree that concerns about the integrity of sports are misplaced? Explain.

Editor's note: The discussion that follows presents common arguments made in support of this perspective, reinforced by facts, quotes, and examples taken from various sources.

Many people both in and out of sports argue that PEDs are a menace and need to be eradicated. These observers offer rationalizations for their positions, rationalizations that on the surface seem reasonable: the health of the athlete, the integrity of the sport. But on close inspection these positions make little sense. The fears are overblown, the concern about integrity misplaced. The reality is that the drive to ban PEDs is doomed to failure. Trying to keep drugs out of sports is impossible and undesirable, and the effort to drive away PED use costs much more time and money than it is worth. Nor is it respectful to grown athletes to try to monitor what they put into their bodies. The world should abandon the effort, stop moralizing about whether records are truly legitimate, and accept the reality that PEDs are, and will continue to be, an important part of sports.

Issues with Drug Testing

One of the biggest reasons for accepting PED use is that drug testing is ineffective. Only a relative handful of athletes are caught doping in any given year. WADA's figures suggest that at most 1 or 2 percent of drug tests are positive. This statistic obviously understates how many actual drug users there are. Passing a drug test, even with a body filled with steroids, HGH, and banned stimulants, is not difficult, and many championship-caliber athletes can attest to the ease of doing so. The East German swimmers of the 1970s never failed a test, for example, but the world now knows that they were on PEDs when they won their Olympic medals. More recently, baseball stars such as infielder Alex Rodriguez and outfielder Gary Sheffield have admitted to PED use—without ever being caught by a drug test. No doubt there are plenty of current athletes who have likewise passed every drug test they have been given but nonetheless use PEDs.

A large part of the issue lies with testing itself. The history of drug testing gives athletes and fans little reason to trust the results. During the 2016 Olympics, for example, drug testers were unable to carry out as many as five hundred of the tests they had scheduled. A WADA report blamed communication issues for the bulk of the problems. "Ultimately many athletes targeted for testing . . . simply could not be found and the mission had to be aborted,"[4] the report read. Other athletes were not tested because drug testers could not find transportation to the testing center.

Doping tests have other problems as well. For one, they are expensive. To administer a single drug test at the Olympics costs an estimated $400. With more than five thousand tests planned for each Summer Olympics, the total bill can easily exceed $2 million. Surely there are better ways to spend that sum of money. In addition, the whole notion of a drug test is demeaning. Athletes in many sports are subjected to random testing, which means they must inform officials of their whereabouts at all times. "Say I'm going to the grocery store to pick up eggs for breakfast," explains US sprinter English Gardner. "But first I have to tag in and tell [the testing organization] I'm going."[5]

Drug tests can also encourage athletes to lie and to blame others for positive tests. Aware that a positive test result may cost them money and awards, many famous athletes will do whatever they can to assert their innocence. In 2011, for instance, a drug test revealed that baseball player Ryan Braun had been using synthetic testosterone, a hormone that builds strength and muscle mass. Braun vehemently denied having used PEDs of any kind and charged that the tester had mishandled the sample. Officials accepted Braun's explanations and decided not to suspend him. In July 2013, however, Braun changed course and admitted the truth: He had indeed used testosterone. "It was a huge mistake for which I am deeply ashamed,"[6] Braun noted.

"Say I'm going to the grocery store to pick up eggs for breakfast. But first I have to tag in and tell [the testing organization] I'm going."[5]

—US runner English Gardner

Drug testing thus creates an environment of lies and suspicion. It diminishes athletes' dignity, costs enormous amounts of money, and cannot even be relied on to find all PED users—not least because the people responsible for carrying out the testing cannot be trusted to do it properly. What, then, is the point of testing for PEDs at all? The sports world would be better served by leaving PED users alone and allowing athletes to use drugs without penalty if that is their choice.

Cheating and Interventions

The ineffectiveness of drug testing is not the only reason why PED use among athletes should be acceptable. Consistency is another. Proponents of drug testing often say that PED use is cheating because drugs such as anabolic steroids and HGH give athletes an unfair advantage. Instead of working to improve themselves, or so the argument goes, athletes rely on modern medical science. There may be some validity to this concern.

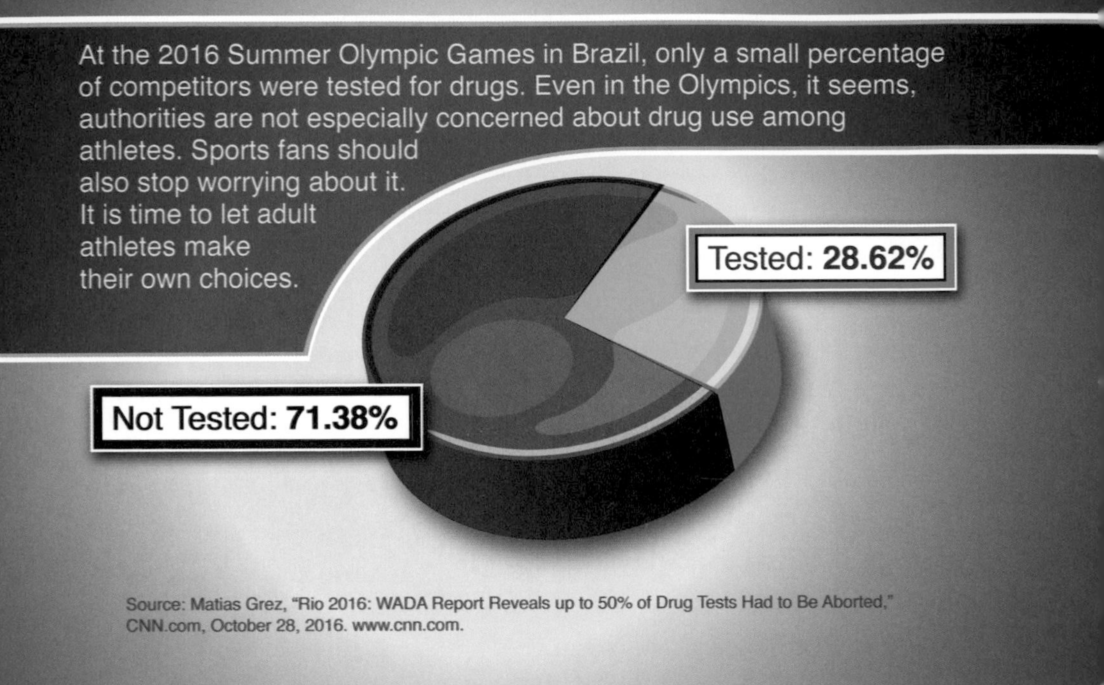

Certainly it is true that lab-created stimulants and banned substances such as EPO represent "quick fixes" that can increase performance with little effort.

But medical interventions are common in the sports world, and it is hypocritical to ban PEDs while accepting medical advances in other ways. One obvious example is LASIK, a type of surgery that corrects nearsightedness. In most sports, having excellent eyesight is a necessity. Should not those who adopt a moralistic approach regarding drugs feel the same way about LASIK? Both PEDs and LASIK, after all, improve the ability of the human body to perform at an extremely high level without demanding much work from the athlete. And yet no anti-doping advocate seems troubled by the prevalence of LASIK procedures among athletes. "If steroids are cheating, why isn't LASIK?"[7] a commentator asks. No one has adequately answered this question.

Nutrition is another example of how advances in medical science can be completely acceptable in some situations, while the use of PEDs is scorned. Over the years scientists have learned a remarkable amount about the dietary needs of the human body. Many top athletes and sports teams have personal chefs and nutritionists who monitor what individual athletes eat, and they serve foods designed to keep their charges in the peak of health. Today, too, most athletes take vitamins and supplements that help them maintain or increase their physical abilities. Modern "smart" exercise equipment and innovative exercise techniques, such as training at high altitude to improve endurance, are still other examples of the unaccountable divide between acceptable uses of medical advances and uses that can get an athlete suspended for months or even years.

"If steroids are cheating, why isn't LASIK?"[7]

—*Slate* writer William Saletan

Nor is it clear that PEDs are as injurious to health as many people assert. Certainly, some PEDs are associated with risks. The medical evidence is clear, for example, that taking anabolic steroids can cause damage to the liver. However, many other PEDs are much more benign. Some researchers argue that HGH, for example, has few serious side effects. And even if all banned substances were truly dangerous, what is gained by telling athletes not to take them? Athletes do not always follow the rules. It would be wiser—and more respectful—to alert competitors to the risks of taking certain drugs and then allow them to make choices like the adults that they are.

Eliminating penalties for PEDs, then, would solve a host of problems. It would save millions of dollars in testing costs, put PEDs on the same footing as other common medical procedures, and do away with a drug testing system that works poorly and creates unnecessary anxiety among athletes and fans. The public should accept the reality of the current situation and stop stigmatizing the achievements of athletes who take PEDs.

PED Use by Athletes Should Not Be Allowed

"If you don't have an even playing field, you lose the foundation of competition. It should be my best against your best, not my best against the best drugs you can covertly use to transform yourself."

—Tom Verducci, a sportswriter for *Sports Illustrated*

Tom Verducci, "How I Decide Who Gets My Hall of Fame Vote, and Why Steroid Users Don't Belong," *Sports Illustrated*, January 10, 2017. www.si.com.

Consider these questions as you read:

1. How effective do you find the argument that PEDs should be unacceptable because they damage an athlete's health? Explain.
2. To what extent do you agree with WADA that sports are or should be primarily about character and values? Why?
3. In what ways is drug use like adding an electric motor to a bicycle? In what ways are the two different?

Editor's note: The discussion that follows presents common arguments made in support of this perspective, reinforced by facts, quotes, and examples taken from various sources.

Many athletes over the years have made the decision to take performance-enhancing drugs. Quite a few of these men and women have been highly successful. With the assistance of steroids, HGH, and banned stimulants, they have won gold medals, world championships, and most valuable player awards. In a few cases, moreover, they have become some of the most recognizable people on the planet. Sprinter Tyson Gay, cyclist Lance Armstrong, and baseball player Mark McGwire all achieved fame based partly on their decision to take drugs. Many other big stars have

PED Users Do Not Belong in the Hall of Fame

Athletes who use performance-enhancing drugs are cheaters—and cheaters do not deserve recognition in the Baseball Hall of Fame. This was the finding of a 2016 Yahoo! Sports survey of 546 American adults who actively follow Major League Baseball. When asked whether players who have been caught or suspected of using PEDs should be allowed into the Hall of Fame, a resounding 69 percent said absolutely not. The message is clear: PED use by athletes is unacceptable.

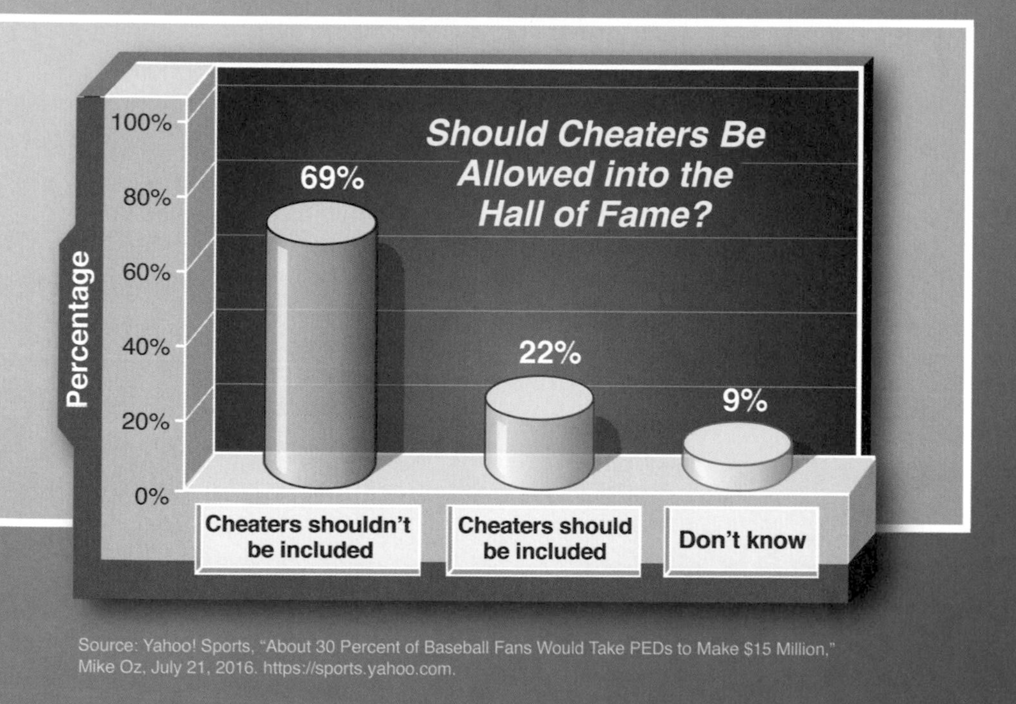

Source: Yahoo! Sports, "About 30 Percent of Baseball Fans Would Take PEDs to Make $15 Million," Mike Oz, July 21, 2016. https://sports.yahoo.com.

been suspected of drug use as well, though proof in these cases is lacking. Nearly all observers would agree that doping has left its mark on the world of sports.

For some observers, the prevalence of PEDs does not appear to be much of a concern. Some even argue that penalties for PEDs should be eliminated and that the sports world should move to full acceptance of drugs. But that would be a disastrous direction to take. Not only do drugs destroy the health of the athletes who take them, but the use of drugs damages the ideals of sport and unfairly denies honest athletes the chance to shine. The process of testing for drugs is not perfect; in particular, the tests are not always as reliable or as effective as they ought to be. But these deficits in no way validate the notion that athletes should be allowed to gobble PEDs as if they were sunflower seeds. No, drugs are an area where sports authorities need to take a stand. There is no justification for removing the penalties attached to drug use.

Health Issues

The first reason for continuing to ban PEDs involves the health of the athlete. Simply put, PEDs are dangerous. Anabolic steroids, perhaps the best known of all PEDs, carry with them a long list of unpleasant and damaging side effects. McGwire was the leading home run hitter in baseball in 1998, connecting for seventy home runs and shattering the previous single-season record of sixty-one. Three years later, he was out of baseball, in large part because steroids had inflated his body to a size greater than his knees could support. McGwire's body, writes author Howard Bryant, became "far too powerful for his frame. McGwire grew so big his joints gave in."[8] Other users report effects such as voice deepening in females, breast development in males, acne on the face and back, anger management issues, and an increased risk of liver cancer and heart problems.

> **"I wobble when I walk and have to hold on to someone for support, and I have trouble remembering things."[9]**
>
> —Football player Lyle Alzado, who believed that steroid use caused his fatal cancer

In a few cases use of steroids has been linked to the death of athletes. Football star Lyle Alzado, for example, died of brain cancer in 1992, just a few weeks past his forty-third birthday. He began taking steroids as a college player in 1969 and continued through his playing career and beyond. Alzado believed that the steroids had brought about the cancer that caused his early death. "Now look at me," he wrote after doctors diagnosed him as terminally ill. "I wobble when I walk and have to hold on to someone for support, and I have trouble remembering things. My last wish? That no one else ever dies this way."[9] The use of anabolic steroids can lead to embarrassing skin conditions and emotional outbursts—and it can also be a killer.

Steroids are among the most dangerous PEDs, but they are hardly the only ones to negatively impact an athlete's health. HGH can lead to arthritis, diabetes, and high blood pressure. Many stimulants increase the risk of stroke and heart issues; they are also addictive. EPO, used by cyclists and other endurance athletes, is particularly hazardous. During the late 1990s at least a dozen young cyclists in Belgium and the Netherlands died of heart attacks after ingesting EPO. Doctors believe that the drug added so many red cells to the cyclists' blood that the liquid became too thick and heavy to pump easily, putting an unbearable strain on the heart. And not all PEDs have been thoroughly tested on healthy adults. There is no telling what medical troubles may surface down the road for athletes who are taking untested drugs in the prime of their careers.

Ethics and Ideals

In addition to the health risks, doping in sports should not be condoned because it is fundamentally unethical. Drugs destroy the ideals of sport. The goal of competition is not, as one newspaper wryly put it, "may the best drugs win."[10] Rather, sport is about athletes, unaided by chemicals, being pitted against one another to see which swimmer completes the designated number of laps first, which archer comes closest to hitting the target, or which diver most impresses the judges. To permit drug use is to throw these time-tested ideals away in favor of a new world of competition in which anything goes. Those competitions might be interesting to watch. But they would not be sport as fans have come to understand it. Sports fans might as well watch a competition between robots.

Indeed, one of the most cherished ideals of sport is fair competition, and the use of PEDs goes against that ideal. Athletes who take drugs are cheating. Running a race against a doped opponent is like playing poker against opponents who keep extra aces in their sleeves. WADA writes that sport is about values, which is undeniable. People speak often of sports instilling character, respect, community, and fair play, among many other virtues, many of which are mentioned in the agency's anti-doping code. None of these values, however, is consistent with the use of drugs, and so a contest between competitors who are doping violates these ideals. "Doping," the WADA concludes, "is fundamentally contrary to the spirit of sport."[11]

In particular, drugs are problematic because in many cases they replace the old-fashioned virtues of perseverance and hard work. Under the current rules, an athlete who wishes to get better at his or her craft must put in enormous amounts of time and energy. The workout regimens of Olympic athletes are astonishing. A top-flight swimmer, for example, may swim thousands of yards a day in addition to weight work, flexibility training, and more. Such intense physical exercise requires a remarkable amount of energy and commitment. With drugs, though, similar results may be achievable with much less work. A gold medal, world championship, or other title should be the result of effort, not needles.

"Doping is fundamentally contrary to the spirit of sport."[11]

—The WADA *World Anti-Doping Code 2015*

Drawing the Line

Allowing PEDs, moreover, would lead to what anti-doping advocate Richard Pound describes as a "vicious circle" in which athletes, free of the need to pass drug tests, take greater and greater quantities of more and more potent drugs. "Instead of taking 10 grams or 10 cc's" of a currently banned substance, argues Pound, "they'll take 20 or 30 or 40." The result, he fears, is that sports will become "increasingly violent, extreme, and meaningless, [and] practiced by a class of chemical and/or genetic mutant gladiators."[12] In short, people who believe that athletes will be content to take small amounts of steroids, stimulants, or testosterone are fooling themselves.

Finally, where should the line be drawn, and why? If it becomes acceptable for cyclists to inject themselves with EPO or fill their bodies with stimulants, would it not be equally acceptable for cyclists to attach electric motors to their bikes? The answer, a sports fan might say, is obvious: Electric motors are antithetical to the spirit of the contest. They would change bicycle races into something very different. This response, of course, confirms that sports are not really about producing the greatest conceivable achievements. Instead, they are about doing as well as possible within the limitations of the rules. Just as cycling is no longer cycling if motors are permissible, sports in general will be robbed of their validity should PEDs be allowed. As Thomas H. Murray puts it, if drugs are made acceptable, "we may lose whatever is most graceful, beautiful, and admirable about sport."[13]

Chapter Two

How Much Do PEDs Actually Improve Performance?

PEDs Substantially Improve Athletic Performance

- There are good medical and scientific reasons to believe that most drugs improve performance.
- Many of the best performances in sports history were achieved by athletes who were using drugs.
- Most athletes who dope agree that PEDs have helped them.

PEDs Do Not Significantly Improve Athletic Performance

- Many great achievements in sports were carried out by athletes believed to be drug free.
- Athletes who dope may overstate the value of drugs.
- The medical evidence for many PEDs suggests that there is less benefit to athletes than is often suspected.

PEDs Substantially Improve Athletic Performance

"I guarantee you that you could stick with the same exact training routine you have now, start taking steroids, and gain more size and strength from it—no extra work required."

—Greg Nuckols, fitness expert and sports scientist

Greg Nuckols, "The Science of Steroids," Stronger by Science, October 8, 2014. www.strongerbyscience.com.

Consider these questions as you read:

1. Do you believe that the effectiveness of PEDs is a justification for their use? Explain.
2. How compelling do you find testimonials from athletes who say that PEDs helped them improve their performance? Why?
3. How might you rebut the argument that many of sports' greatest achievements were set by people known to be on drugs?

Editor's note: The discussion that follows presents common arguments made in support of this perspective, reinforced by facts, quotes, and examples taken from various sources.

To choose to take PEDs represents a major risk for an athlete. The medical hazards of substances such as EPO and anabolic steroids are well known, and athletes who ingest these substances know that they may be damaging their health both now and in the future. Since PEDs are banned, moreover, athletes who choose to use them know that they could be caught and penalized, potentially destroying their reputation and livelihood. Athletes who take these drugs, then, will only do so if they believe that PEDs will help them in competition. Because so many athletes from different countries and in different sports make the choice to take PEDs, it is reasonable to assume that these drugs do indeed improve an athlete's performance.

Other evidence, too, supports this conclusion. Some of the greatest athletes of the past half-century are now known to have been using drugs when they compiled their most impressive achievements. And medical research indicates that many banned substances do indeed work to increase an athlete's speed, strength, or stamina. Taken together, the conclusion is inescapable: Performance-enhancing drugs function exactly as their name implies.

Science and Medicine

One very good argument in favor of the effectiveness of PEDs comes from medical research. The known effects of many PEDs are consistent with gains in athletic ability. Anabolic steroids, for example, have been shown to increase strength, both in chronically ill people and in healthy adults. In a recent study, investigators put test subjects on a ten-week regimen of steroids and discovered that the subjects' bodies became noticeably more muscular. It is easy to see how this extra muscle growth would translate to sports. Greater muscle power would allow a sprinter to explode out of the starting blocks, permit a swimmer to keep up an intense pace for longer than other competitors, or let a batter hit a baseball harder and farther. Given what we know about the effects of steroids on the body, it would be a surprise if they did not increase athletic performance.

"Besides making muscles bigger, anabolic steroids may help athletes recover from a hard workout more quickly by reducing the muscle damage that occurs during the session."[14]

—The Mayo Clinic

There is evidence, too, that steroids speed up the process of injury recovery. "Besides making muscles bigger," notes the world-famous Mayo Clinic, a Minnesota organization known for its medical expertise, "anabolic steroids may help athletes recover from a hard workout more quickly by reducing the muscle damage that occurs during the session. This enables athletes to work out harder and more frequently without overtraining."[14] Indeed, many former PED users agree that taking steroids enabled them to work

Steroids Gave Mark McGwire a Home Run Boost

Baseball slugger Mark McGwire hit forty-nine home runs in 1987, his first full season. In the early 1990s McGwire's home run totals dropped, partly because he missed games because of injuries. Beginning about 1994, McGwire has stated, he started taking regular doses of steroids—and he quickly began hitting record levels of home runs. Clearly PEDs improve athletic performance.

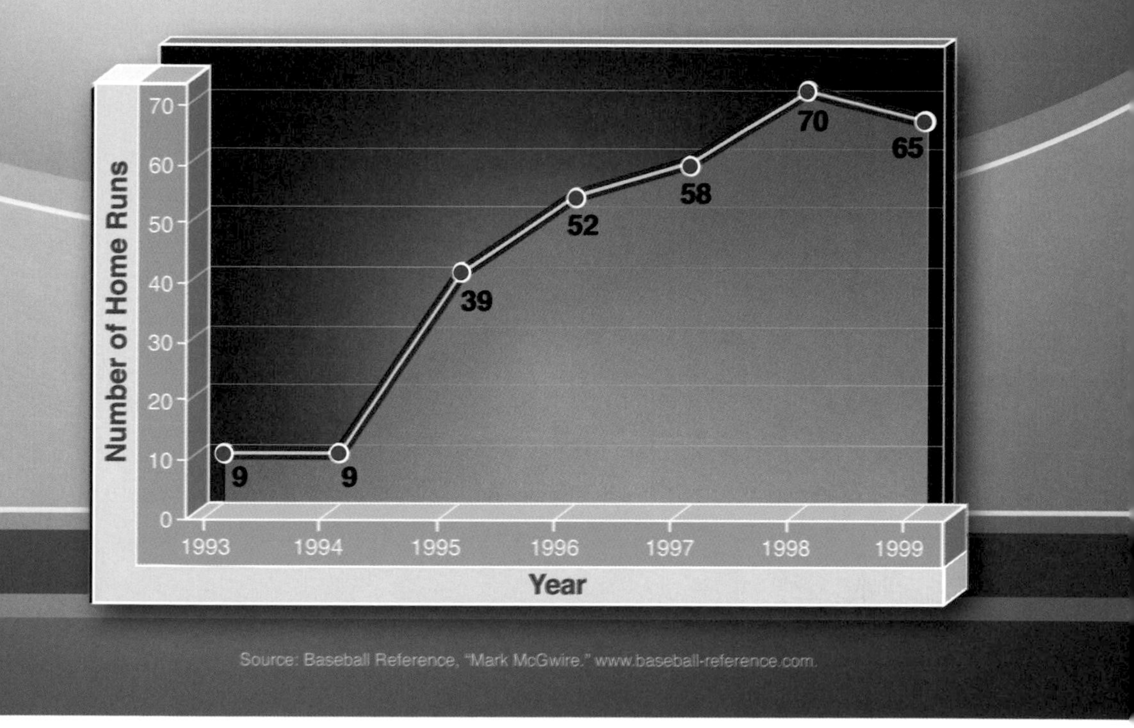

Source: Baseball Reference, "Mark McGwire." www.baseball-reference.com.

harder and longer even while taking fewer rest breaks. Again, it would be peculiar indeed if there were no corresponding improvements in the performance of these athletes.

These benefits are not limited to steroids. Lab studies reveal, for example, that stimulants generally make people more alert, less weary, and better able to focus. An auto racer, basketball player, or football star under the influence of stimulants, then, can be expected to speed up his or her reaction time and maintain an energetic state throughout an athletic contest. That can only help improve athletic performance. EPO has the effect of increasing the body's production of red blood cells, which also provides a boost to athletic ability. "More red cells carrying oxygen around your body means increased aerobic potential,"[15] points out Charlotte Cowie, a doctor who works with the United Kingdom's Olympic team. Again, the conclusion is evident: Drug usage leads to gains in athletic performance.

East Germany's Swim Team

The reality, moreover, is that many of the sports world's greatest records were the work of athletes who were taking PEDs. One of the first examples of the power of PEDs was the women's swimming team from East Germany during the 1970s. Through the early 1970s East Germany had not done especially well during Olympic swimming competitions. The East German women's team won just five medals in 1972, for example, none of them gold. But in 1976 that changed. Led by sprint specialist Kornelia Ender, East German women finished first in eleven of the thirteen events and added six silver medals and a bronze as well.

East German coaches attributed the women's sudden success to new training methods and hard work on the part of the athletes. In fact, East Germany had developed training academies highly focused on developing young talent. But observers from Western countries doubted that training methods and motivated athletes could be the entire story. Richard Pound, a former competitive swimmer who is now an anti-doping advocate, remembered being struck by the sheer size of the East German women athletes in at the 1976 Olympics. "I could stand behind Kornelia Ender and you couldn't see around her," he recalled. "These women were just enormous."[16]

The East German medalists passed their drug tests without difficulty, however, and so most observers kept their doubts to themselves. But those who questioned the East German achievements were eventually proved correct. In 1991, soon after East Germany was reunified with West Germany, documents surfaced describing an East German state-run doping program in which athletes were routinely given anabolic steroids and other PEDs. Before long, former coaches and athletes from

East Germany confirmed the truth. East German scientists had developed drugs that increased the muscle mass and strength of athletes, particularly women; and most if not all of the 1976 East German medalists had been using drugs. Morally, of course, the East Germans were in the wrong. Their swimmers were cheating. But for many observers in the sports world, the true message of East Germany's success had nothing to do with ethics. It was, instead, that steroids are effective.

Records and Anecdotes

The East Germans were not alone in their recognition of the power of PEDs. A remarkable number of the world's most impressive athletic achievements were fueled by drugs. At the 1988 Olympics in South Korea, Canadian sprinter Ben Johnson completed the 100-meter dash in a world-record 9.79 seconds—only to be stripped of his medal when his drug test revealed that he had used steroids. Cyclist Lance Armstrong's unprecedented string of seven consecutive first-place finishes in the grueling Tour de France, likewise, was accomplished in part because of Armstrong's decision to take EPO, testosterone, and other PEDs. Barry Bonds, who holds baseball's career and single-season home run records, has admitted to taking steroids (though he asserts that his trainer gave them to him without telling him what they were). Each of these athletes would likely not have achieved at the same level without drugs.

"I knew that steroids would improve my stamina and keep me healthy and explosive throughout the long baseball season."[17]

—Baseball player Jose Canseco

The prevalence of drug-aided records strongly points to the effectiveness of drugs. Anecdotally, too, athletes at all levels of competition have noticed improvements—often sudden improvements—in their physical abilities soon after embarking on a regimen of PED use. Star baseball player Jose Canseco, who used steroids through most of his career, has been vocal in attributing his success not just to hard work but also to the boost he got from PEDs. "I knew that steroids would improve my stamina,"

Canseco wrote, "and keep me healthy and explosive throughout the long baseball season."[17] American sprinter Kelli White agrees, noting that her sudden improvement in performance was caused in large part by drugs. "In a relatively short period," she explains, "I had gone from being a very competitive sprinter to being the fastest woman in the world."[18] Perhaps former National Football League (NFL) player Lyle Alzado said it best: "I outran, outhit, outanythinged everybody," he reported. "All along I was taking steroids, and I saw that they made me play better and better."[19] Science, the record books, and the words of the athletes themselves all are in agreement, then: Drugs work.

PEDs Do Not Significantly Improve Athletic Performance

"I tried [steroids] when I was eighteen, me and my football buddies. Nothing happened."

—Athlete and actor Dwayne "the Rock" Johnson

Quoted in Stephen Galloway, "The Drive (and Despair) of the Rock," *Hollywood Reporter*, June 18, 2014. www.hollywoodreporter.com.

Consider these questions as you read:

1. How compelling do you find testimonials from athletes who say that drugs did not help them? Why?
2. How might you rebut the conclusions offered in the Hermann-Henneberg study, which found that PEDs make no difference in an athlete's performance?
3. How convincing do you find the argument about the placebo effect and the effectiveness of drugs in sports? Explain.

Editor's note: The discussion that follows presents common arguments made in support of this perspective, reinforced by facts, quotes, and examples taken from various sources.

The notion that PEDs improve athletic ability has become solidly entrenched in sports. But in fact, there is room for plenty of debate about the actual value of banned substances on athletes. Contrary to popular opinion, the record books do not show that PEDs are effective. Neither do the personal experiences of athletes who have doped. Even scientific evidence is a good deal less definitive than many people believe. The truth is that PEDs most likely have a small effect, at best, on athletic skills. Sports fans, coaches, and athletes alike should be wary of assertions that PEDs routinely and significantly boost the skills of athletes.

Clean Record Holders

Those who argue for the efficacy of drugs typically point to sports record books as evidence that doping works. They are certainly correct that several well-publicized achievements belong to athletes known today to have been using drugs while setting these marks. What this argument ignores, however, is that many remarkable records over the years were set by people who most likely were *not* involved with PEDs. Former New York Yankees relief pitcher Mariano Rivera, for example, is widely hailed as the greatest relief pitcher ever; but as a newspaper notes, "Rivera has never been linked to any PED use."[20]

The same is true of famous and successful athletes such as tennis star Roger Federer, Olympic swimmer Katie Ledecky, and Green Bay Packers quarterback Aaron Rodgers. It is impossible to be certain that these athletes have never taken PEDs, but nothing in their personal or professional lives suggests that they have. Their success indicates that it is possible to be quite good at a sport without using PEDs. In fact, given the feats of athletes like Ledecky—who won four gold medals and a silver medal during the 2016 Olympics, setting two world records in the process—it seems clear that athletes who do not dope can even come to dominate their sports. If PEDs were truly as effective as people believe, the Riveras and Federers of the sports world would be beaten badly at every turn by drug users. But that is not the case. It seems odd to conclude, then, that PEDs are as effective as many observers think.

Another problem with the argument is exemplified by baseball player Barry Bonds. Bonds, whose best years coincided with the seasons when he was doping, is often cited as an athlete whose PED-aided performance reveals the effectiveness of drugs. But the evidence does not support that conclusion. In reality, Bonds was a tremendous player long before he began using PEDs. Before 1998, the year most sources agree that Bonds's drug use began, Bonds won three most valuable player awards, was a frequent selection to his league's All-Star team, and had been given the most lucrative contract to that point in the history of baseball. "Bonds already had performed like a Hall of Famer,"[21] writes sports commentator Dave Brown. The gaudy statistics of Bonds's greatest seasons are not out of line with the rest of his career. PEDs had less to do with his best years than many assume.

Studies and Anecdotes

Nor is Bonds an outlier. Australian researchers Aaron Hermann and Maciej Henneberg published a study in 2014 in which they concluded that PEDs make no difference in an athlete's performance. Hermann and Henneberg looked at competitors in twenty-six Olympic events over time and divided them into two categories: those known to have doped and those believed to have been clean. "The average best life records for 'doped' top athletes," Hermann notes, "did not differ significantly from those considered not to have doped."[22] Additionally, Hermann and Henneberg point out that performances in these events have improved relatively little over the years. And of course any improvements may be attributable to better training methods, better nutrition, and better equipment, rather than to drug use.

Anecdotal evidence from players, similarly, does not show a clear connection between doping and athletic success. For one, not all athletes report improvement when they begin taking drugs. Baseball player Fernando Viña says that HGH did not make him a better player. Tony Gwynn, who says he never took PEDs in his Hall of Fame career but who played with and against several steroid users, came to the same conclusion. "Steroids do not guarantee you're going to have success," he said soon after his retirement from baseball. "I think a lot of people think that they will, but they don't."[23]

> **"The average best life records for 'doped' top athletes did not differ significantly from those considered not to have doped."[22]**
>
> —Researcher Aaron Hermann

It is wise, moreover, to be at least somewhat skeptical of athletes who say that doping helped build their skills. One reason is the placebo effect, which is the tendency of people to believe that a pill or other medication is effective even when it has no actual medicinal value. In one case from the 1990s, French cyclist Richard Virenque asked a trainer named Willy Voet to inject him with stimulants before a race. "God I felt good!" Virenque exclaimed after completing the ride. "That stuff's just amazing."[24] What Virenque did not know was that Voet had

PEDs Are Common but Running Times Show Little Improvement

Everyone knows that today's athletes use performance-enhancing drugs. So one would expect to see dramatically improved times for track events. But this is not the case. In the last few decades, winning times in most track events have improved only by small amounts. The gold medal time in the women's 100-meter sprint, for example, was just 0.29 seconds faster in 2016 than it had been nearly half a century earlier, in 1968. If drugs were truly effective, one would expect to see much greater improvement. Such minimal change suggests that drugs do not have much effect on athletic performance.

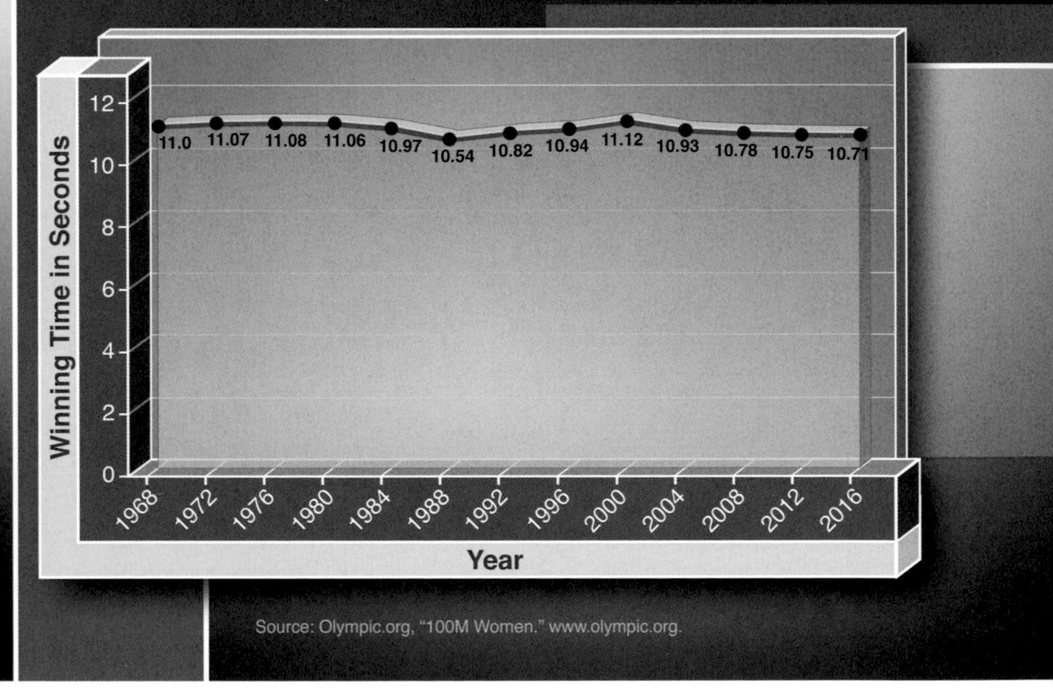

Source: Olympic.org, "100M Women." www.olympic.org.

not actually injected Virenque with the stimulant but rather with glucose. Virenque's success that day was due not to drugs but to his belief that drugs would benefit him.

Medical Evidence

Finally, physiological evidence has by no means established that PEDs work. For many of the most popular PEDs, in fact, studies suggest that the drugs are largely ineffective. HGH is one example. Wrestlers, boxers, and numerous other athletes have taken HGH, but as far as science is concerned, they have done so in vain. "Most clinical studies suggest that HGH won't help an athlete at all," points out journalist Daniel Engber. While HGH may increase muscle mass and reduce body fat in ordinary people, high-level athletes are already muscular enough that adding HGH makes little if any difference. "A chiseled physique won't help you hit a baseball or throw a punch,"[25] Engber notes.

EPO is another example of a banned substance that may not actually have much effect in top athletes. In theory, EPO ought to improve athletic performance. Adding red blood cells should increase the body's ability to bring oxygen to muscles, thereby allowing athletes to run, pedal, or swim at a faster rate and for a longer time. When EPO is tested on athletes, though, the results are not as expected. A 2017 study found that cyclists who were given EPO did not perform better in road races than cyclists given a sugar pill.

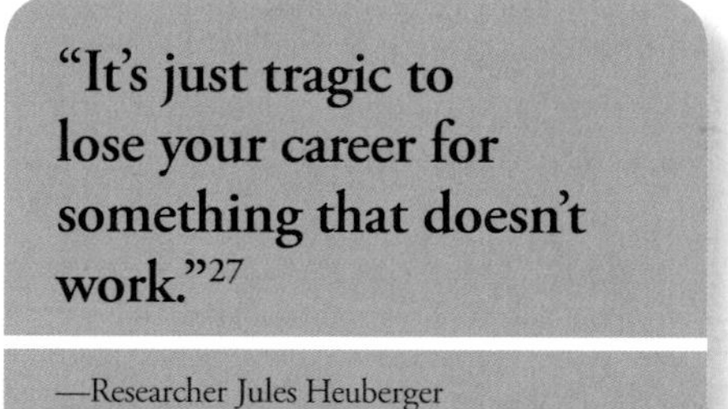

Even the extra muscle mass acquired by steroid users may not improve performance in most sports. "We assume that, if you are stronger, you will perform better, but that might not necessarily be true," says researcher Michael Bahrke, who studies steroids. "For football and baseball players, explosive muscle mass might relate to more power, but it is difficult to document that it leads to better performance."[26] Given the medical evidence and the experiences of people like Bonds, Virenque, and Gwynn, people who follow sports should not be quick to accept that drugs automatically improve performance. It is much more likely that any boost from PEDs are small. As Dutch drug researcher Jules Heuberger notes, referring to Lance Armstrong's punishment for using EPO, "It's just tragic to lose your career for something that doesn't work."[27]

Chapter Three

Does Testing for PED Use Deter Athletes from Doping?

PED Testing Deters Drug Use

- Positive drug tests lead to suspensions, loss of income, and public humiliation.
- Athletes avoid using drugs because they fear being caught by testing if they do use PEDs.
- Passing a drug test is not a given for an athlete who is using PEDs.

PED Testing Does Not Deter Drug Use

- Even when drug testing catches high-profile athletes, others continue to engage in doping.
- It can be easy for athletes to pass drug tests even if they are using PEDs.
- Top-flight athletes as a group have different motivations and priorities than ordinary people.

PED Testing Deters Drug Use

"If student/athletes are on notice that they may be tested at any time, they're less likely to use drugs."

—Mary Wilfert, National Collegiate Athletic Association associate director of health and safety

Quoted in Chris Wagner, "NCAA: Drug-Testing Policies, Suspicions Offer Strong Deterrents," *Syracuse.com* (blog), March 6, 2012. http://blog.syracuse.com.

Consider these questions as you read:

1. In your opinion, what would be the worst effect of failing a drug test for an athlete? Explain.
2. Which argument in this section do you find most compelling and which least compelling? Explain.
3. Do you agree that failed drug tests are much more serious issues for athletes than simple rumors and accusations? Why or why not?

Editor's note: The discussion that follows presents common arguments made in support of this perspective, reinforced by facts, quotes, and examples taken from various sources.

Very little rocks the sports world like the revelation that a famous and successful athlete has been accused of taking drugs. Tennis fans and players were astonished in 2016, for example, when the news broke that Maria Sharapova had tested positive for a banned substance. Similarly, the PED use by well-known athletes like cyclist Lance Armstrong is typically covered for months in newspapers, magazines, and television shows. Even rumors that an athlete is doping can create quite a commotion among sports fans, commentators, and other competitors. In early 2017, for example, reports began to circulate that British track star Mo Farah, the winner of four Olympic gold medals, had been using drugs. As of September 2017, searching for "Mo Farah drugs" on the Internet returned more than 4 million results.

Drug Tests Deter PED Use

The World Anti-Doping Agency has amassed statistics on the number of positive drug tests recorded in various sports. Based on 2014 data, less than 2 percent of drug tests come up positive even in sports well-known for drug use—notably cycling, track and field, and weight lifting. This suggests that the great majority of athletes are clean—probably because they know that if they cheat they will be caught and disciplined.

Sport	Total Tests	Positive Tests	Percentage of Tests That Are Positive
Weight Lifting	8,806	169	1.9
Golf	507	8	1.6
Boxing	4,258	55	1.3
Wrestling	5,154	60	1.2
Tae Kwon Do	2,034	22	1.1
Track and Field	25,830	261	1.0
Cycling	22,471	221	1.0

Note: All other sports had positive rates of less than 1 percent.

Source: Bonnie Berkowitz and Tim Meko, "Stronger. Faster. Longer. And Higher," *Washington Post*, June 28, 2016. www.washingtonpost.com.

From the perspective of an athlete, not much can be worse than testing positive for PEDs. A positive test will cost the athlete dearly in several different ways. For one, athletes who are found to be doping usually must serve a suspension before being allowed to compete again. The length of the suspension varies by sport, of course, and may be reduced upon appeal but is often as long as two years. Even leagues that have relatively light penalties for first-time drug offenders, such as the NFL, typically force players to sit out a quarter of the season.

The inability to compete is bad enough, but a positive drug test often has a strong financial impact on athletes as well. Players in North

American team sports are generally suspended without pay, which can mean forfeiting a substantial amount of money. In 2017, for example, National Basketball Association player Joakim Noah's twenty-game doping suspension cost him more than $3 million in salary. Endorsement deals, which can be exceptionally lucrative, are also at risk when an athlete is found to have been doping. Sharapova's suspension for PEDs caused several of her sponsors to drop their contracts with her temporarily. One, watchmaker TAG Heuer, decided not to renew the relationship even after Sharapova's suspension came to an end. Not counting lost income from tournament play, Sharapova's suspension likely cost her millions of dollars in lost sponsor fees.

Embarrassment and Shame

In addition, athletes who are caught doping experience sharply negative treatment from fans and media outlets. Baseball players Rafael Palmeiro, Mark McGwire, and Barry Bonds have not been voted into their sport's Hall of Fame despite strong credentials; some voters state clearly that these players' drug use is the reason. If Bonds and other suspected drug users get in, charges columnist Pat Caputo, the Hall of Fame "would become the Hall of Shame."[28] News personality Piers Morgan called Lance Armstrong a "snivelling, lying, cheating little wretch"[29] after the cyclist admitted to using PEDs after years of denial. And the news that baseball player Alex Rodriguez had taken drugs was met with a barrage of headlines that blared "A-Roid"[30] (a play on his nickname of A-Rod), doctored photographs showing Rodriguez with impossibly bulging muscles, and cartoons of him holding a syringe instead of a bat.

> **"[He is a] snivelling, lying, cheating little wretch."[29]**
>
> —Television personality Piers Morgan on Lance Armstrong

Besides losing money and the ability to compete, athletes who are found to be doping are publicly shamed for their decision. Just as no athlete would voluntarily choose to sit out a season or two at the cost of millions of dollars in earnings, no athlete would choose to be held up to ridicule and embarrassment. Thus, it stands to reason that the consequences of using PEDs would make a sports figure think twice about taking banned hormones, stimulants, or other substances. In particular, they will strive not to fail a drug test. While athletes have successfully pushed back against rumors and accusations of doping, it is much more difficult to argue against a positive drug test. In this way, drug tests clearly act as a deterrent to athletes who are considering taking PEDs.

As a matter of fact, the possibility of failing a test may be the only thing that will deter an athlete who is determined to improve his or her performance. Consider a world in which there is no testing whatever. What will prevent athletes from doping? The answer, clearly, is nothing. Without drug tests, there is no way to penalize people who take PEDs, and without any mechanism to punish PED users, it is reasonable to believe that athletes will ingest whatever they can get. At the same time, not every athlete is using drugs. One reason why some athletes abstain is likely to be the existence of drug testing.

Effectiveness of Tests

Those who believe that drug tests do not deter PED use do make some valid points. One of these points is that many competitors who dope are never caught by drug tests. Lance Armstrong, after all, used to say that he passed more than five hundred drug tests in his career without ever failing one. That is an unfortunate reality. Drugmakers find it easy to stay a step ahead of the drug testers by creating new drugs that do not show up in standard blood or urine tests. That too is unfortunate but true. And some athletes, trainers, and coaches have found ways of getting around the tests, such as by surreptitiously exchanging a doper's urine sample for a sample given by a person who does not use PEDs. Clearly, drug testing is not infallible.

The truth, however, is that drug testing does work. The list of athletes who have been caught by drug tests is both long and impressive. In 2016 and 2017, for example, famous athletes who tested positive included Noah, Sharapova, and baseball outfielder Starling Marte, among others. In one sense, positive tests represent the dark side of sports. They indicate, after all, the presence of cheaters among the ranks of athletes. But positive tests also stand for something good. They are an indication that systematic testing can and do catch athletes who dope. When tests nab high-profile athletes such as Sharapova and Noah, other athletes will think twice about filling their bodies with drugs.

> **"You have to know what goes into your body and the consequences. We have to have a deterrent."[32]**
>
> —Tennis player Roger Federer

There is evidence, in fact, that athletes are scared away from drugs when they see other competitors fail doping tests. "It's a deterrent," Los Angeles Angels pitcher Matt Shoemaker said flatly about Marte's positive test and subsequent suspension. "That's why we have so much testing. Guys don't want that in the game."[31] Others agree. "For me, zero tolerance is the best solution," says tennis star Roger Federer, supporting the decision to suspend Sharapova for PED use. "You have to know what goes into your body and the consequences. We have to have a deterrent."[32] That deterrent can only be the threat of a drug test that might reveal that an athlete is doping. Nothing else will work to deter athletes intent on doping—but the possibility of a positive test can do exactly that.

PED Testing Does Not Deter Drug Use

"Testing programmes—as a strategy to detect and deter doping—are no great deterrent for many athletes."

—Marie Overbye, Danish university lecturer in sport management

Marie Overbye, "Deterrence by Risk of Detection? An Inquiry into How Elite Athletes Perceive the Deterrent Effect of the Doping Testing Regime in Their Sport," *Drugs: Education, Prevention and Policy*, July 1, 2016. www.tandfonline.com.

Consider these questions as you read:

1. To what extent do you think that athletes are truly different from ordinary people?
2. Of the arguments given in this section, which do you think most clearly explains the desire of athletes to take drugs despite the risk of testing positive? Why?
3. Under what circumstances, if any, do you think drug testing could become an effective deterrent to drug use? Explain.

Editor's note: The discussion that follows presents common arguments made in support of this perspective, reinforced by facts, quotes, and examples taken from various sources.

One of the biggest stories in the 1988 Summer Olympics involved Canadian sprinter Ben Johnson. In a much-anticipated matchup with American runner Carl Lewis, Johnson not only finished first in the men's 100-meter dash, he set a new world record as well. Johnson was quickly elevated to the status of national hero in Canada. But his reign was short. Two days after the race, the news broke that Johnson had failed his post-competition drug test. His urine sample had tested positive for a steroid called stanozolol. Johnson protested his innocence, but to no avail. He returned home in disgrace, his gold medal was given to Lewis, and his time was stricken from the official record of the year's Olympics.

The story of Ben Johnson is a cautionary tale indeed. His rise and fall was played out on a world stage and was compressed into a matter of hours. Immediately after his apparent victory, Canadian newspapers lauded Johnson with jubilant phrases like "Bentastic"; two days later, he was referred to as "Canada's shame." Even today, years later, Johnson reports that he has not been allowed to get past the mistake he made. "There's people who murder and rape people, go to jail and get out," he told a reporter. "I just break the rules in sport and I've been nailed to the cross."[33]

> **"There's people who murder and rape people, go to jail and get out. I just break the rules in sport and I've been nailed to the cross."[33]**
>
> —Former sprinter Ben Johnson, who tested positive for a steroid in 1988

Johnson's experience provides an important perspective on the question of whether drug testing is an effective deterrent to athletes who are considering taking PEDs. If anything would scare an athlete away from taking drugs, the example of Johnson's well-publicized fall from grace would seem to be it. Athletes of the late 1980s who were on the fence about doping would have seen what happened to Johnson, and they should have taken it to heart. If drug tests were an effective deterrent, one would expect to see drug use by athletes fall off sharply following Johnson's punishment at the Olympics.

Failed Tests and More Doping

But that, of course, is not what happened. In the wake of the revelations about Johnson, doping continued—and by most accounts the level of doping actually increased. In 1989 another athlete from Canada, hurdler Julie Baumann, was suspended for two years for use of stanozolol—the same drug that brought Johnson down. In 1990, just two years after Johnson returned home in disgrace, American track and field athletes Butch Reynolds and Randy Barnes were sanctioned for positive urine

Olympics Doping Violations Increase Despite Testing

Drug testing of Olympic athletes has been going on for years. Despite those tests—and heightened attention to both doping and testing—violations are increasing. Between 1968 and 2012 there have been slight fluctuations, but the overall trend shows an increase in doping violations for both male and female athletes. Clearly, drug testing is not deterring athletes from using performance-enhancing drugs.

Athletes Disqualified After Testing Positive For a Banned Substance, Summer Olympics, by Host City

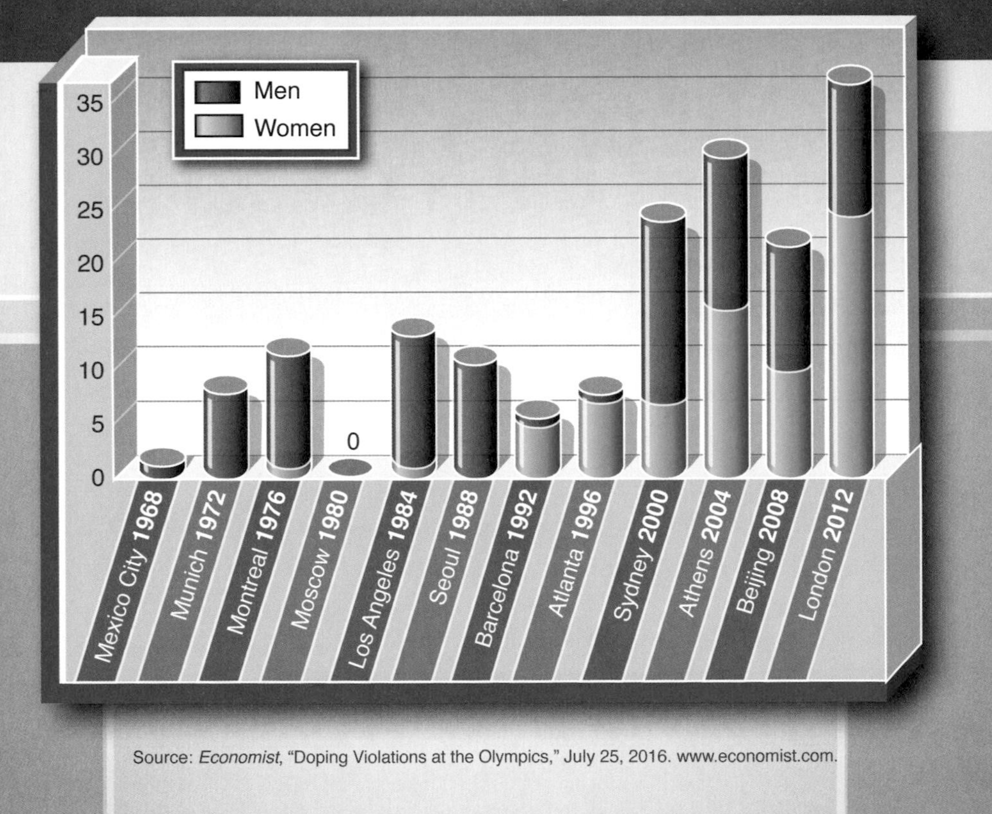

Source: *Economist*, "Doping Violations at the Olympics," July 25, 2016. www.economist.com.

tests. "Doping infractions occurred; there is no doubt, none at all,"[34] explained a doctor involved with the drug tests, dismissing Reynolds's claim that the results were incorrect. It is difficult to look at these and other suspensions and conclude that Johnson's positive drug test made any athlete of the period think twice about taking drugs.

Nor were the late 1980s and early 1990s unusual in this way. Throughout the past few decades, the record is clear: When an athlete is caught and humiliated for doping, others blithely continue their drug-using ways. In 2005, in a much-publicized case, baseball star Rafael Palmeiro failed a drug test and was suspended. Palmeiro's case did not put an end to doping in baseball, though. During the next two years, ten of Palmeiro's fellow Major League Baseball (MLB) players failed drug tests themselves and were consequently suspended. No doubt many other baseball players continued to dope during that time without ever failing a test. Even as penalties became stiffer, failed drug tests still did not deter players from using PEDs. In 2016 New York Mets pitcher Jenrry Mejía failed his third drug test, leading to a lifetime ban from the sport. Did that bring an end to PED use in baseball? It did not. Later that same year, drug tests identified seven more MLB players who were doping.

> **"Elite athletes are different from the general public, especially on desire to win."[37]**
>
> —A 2009 study comparing top-level athletes to nonathletes

To say that drug testing provides any sort of deterrent flies in the face of the evidence. Athletes seem to ignore the negative experiences of those caught by positive drug tests. Perhaps this is because many athletes believe that they will never test positive. Certainly, many observers have a low opinion of the ability of drug testing to identify cheaters. Drugs are constantly evolving, with unethical scientists creating so-called designer drugs that cannot be detected by standard measures. When authorities redesign the drug tests to pick up on those substances, drugmakers simply turn to something new. "Drug testing is . . . impotent, [and] has been impotent since it started,"[35] says Charles Yesalis, an authority on sports medicine and doping.

And even if drug tests were more effective, many athletes have ways of reducing their chances of testing positive. Steroids, once taken largely by mouth or injection, are now often taken via a gel or a patch, methods that leave fewer traces of the material in the body. A second tactic is micro-dosing, or taking regular small doses of certain drugs. Regular low doses may evade detection in drug tests while still providing a boost to the athlete. "Can athletes micro-dose with EPO and testosterone and get away with it?" asks Victor Conte, who was sent to prison for providing PEDs to many professional athletes. "Yes, they can."[36] Using a much less high-tech solution, some athletes have even been known to run away from drug testers when they are subjected to random testing. A Russian athlete did exactly that in early 2016 upon seeing a drug official arrive at a competition.

How Elite Athletes Think

To fully understand why drug testing is not a good deterrent for athletes, however, it is necessary to understand the mind-set of a typical top athlete. Many people who spend time with world-class athletes are struck by their drive, their competitiveness, and their single-minded attention to improving their abilities. Elite athletes are hyperfocused on the next workout and the next event. To them, very little else matters; most of their time and energy go to making small improvements in their technique and tactics. Top athletes are obsessed with being the fastest, the strongest, and the best. They hate to lose, and many will do almost anything to win.

The inclination to push the boundaries is perhaps most notable where PEDs are concerned. Time and again, elite athletes have been willing to take drugs at great risk to their livelihoods—and sometimes to their lives. During the 1980s a researcher named Bob Goldman asked Olympic athletes if they would take a drug that would guarantee them a gold medal—but would also be certain to kill them within five years. More than half of the athletes said they would take the drug. Similar questioning at regular intervals since then has produced similar results. In contrast, a follow-up study in 2009 asked nonathletes whether they would take a drug that guaranteed them success in their field at the cost of their lives. Just 2 of the 250 people polled said they would. "Elite athletes," the study concluded, "are different from the general public, especially on desire to win."[37]

Given results like these, it is unrealistic to expect that drug testing would be a deterrent to most elite athletes. These men and women are focused on improving their skills and preoccupied with winning, to a degree that ordinary people cannot easily comprehend. If these athletes are inclined to take drugs, they will do so regardless of the possibility that they might die as a result; the goal of winning that gold medal is so important. Given that even certain death is not a deterrent to drug use, why would anyone believe that a mere drug test would stop an athlete?

Chapter Four

Are Penalties for PED Use Inconsistent and Unfair?

Penalties for PED Use Are Inconsistent and Unfair

- Athletes from powerful nations are treated differently than athletes representing smaller countries.
- Big stars are often not sufficiently penalized for drug use.
- Different sports, leagues, and events do not punish athletes in the same way for the same infractions.

Penalties for PED Use Are Generally Consistent and Fair

- Star athletes, like other athletes, are heavily penalized for PED use.
- Guidelines for different sports are becoming more consistent.
- An overemphasis on consistency does not always lead to the fairest approach to punishment.

Penalties for PED Use Are Inconsistent and Unfair

"It's a school-by-school patchwork of policies and penalties: A first-time steroid infraction would bench a Florida player for half the season but cost a Texas A&M player only a single game."

—Sharon Terlep, writer for the *Wall Street Journal*

Sharon Terlep, "The NCAA's Drug Problem," *Wall Street Journal*, March 24, 2015. www.wsj.com.

Consider these questions as you read:

1. What is the best evidence given in this section for the argument that penalties are unfair? Why?
2. Can the problem of unfair and inconsistent penalties be solved within the world of sports, or does the problem lie in society? Explain.
3. If penalties cannot be made fair and consistent, should they be eliminated or kept? Why?

Editor's note: The discussion that follows presents common arguments made in support of this perspective, reinforced by facts, quotes, and examples taken from various sources.

If drug testing is to be effective in limiting or eliminating PED use among athletes, then the process of testing must be entirely aboveboard. In particular, penalties for positive tests must be applied in an equitable and evenhanded way. Unfortunately, penalties for positive drug tests vary enormously, depending on the sport, the competition, the league, and the individual athlete. It is difficult to have faith in a system that allows athletes to be treated differently according to who they are. A system of punishment that provides wildly different outcomes for different athletes is inconsistent, discriminatory, and unfair—and in the end, illegitimate.

Russia in the Olympics

One of the strongest arguments that PED penalties are applied inconsistently comes from the Olympic Games. In 2014 investigators found proof that Russian sports authorities were engaged in a state-sponsored program of doping. Faced with the evidence, several Russian leaders acknowledged the government's role in providing athletes with drugs. They promised to end the program and take steps to ensure that Russia's athletes were clean. "Russia fully supports fighting doping,"[38] the country's sports minister promised. Nonetheless, some of the abuses continued. In June 2016, shortly before the Olympics in Brazil, the International Association of Athletics Federations unanimously voted to keep the Russian track team out of the Olympics. But just days before the Olympics began, the International Olympic Committee (IOC) decided to open the Olympics to the Russian team, excluding only those who had failed a drug test at some point during their careers.

> **"[According to the International Olympic Committee] there are nations, and there are 'important nations.'"[41]**
>
> —Journalist Richard Hinds, referring to the Russian doping scandal

Many observers were appalled by the decision to allow Russia to compete. Representatives of the world's leading national anti-doping agencies called the Russian program of PEDs "one of the biggest scandals in sports history"[39] and urged the Olympics to hold Russia accountable unless it changed its ways dramatically. In particular, many observers argued, the Russians should be forced to sit out the 2018 Winter Olympics in South Korea. "We have serious doubts that the 2018 Games will be clean," the agencies announced in a 2017 statement. "A country's sport leaders and organisations should not be given credentials to the Olympics when they intentionally violate the rules and rob clean athletes."[40]

As of early fall 2017, though, the IOC has not acted to remove Russia from the 2018 Olympic Games. Perhaps the IOC is afraid of offending Russia, which after all is an influential nation with a long history of Olympic success. The decision might also be driven by money; Russian broadcasters will pay much more for the right to televise an Olympics that includes Russian athletes than one that excludes them. Whatever the reasons, the result is that Russia will essentially go unpunished for its actions. The Russian government cheated deserving athletes out of medals, risked their own athletes' health, and made a mockery of the attempt to eliminate the scourge of PEDs—and nonetheless continues to participate on the world's biggest athletic stage. Clearly, the IOC has two sets of standards where drug testing is concerned. "There is the IOC in a nut shell," writes journalist Richard Hinds. "There are nations, and there are 'important nations.'"[41] Of course, having two sets of rules is indefensible.

Baseball and Cycling

Olympic athletes from large and powerful countries are not the only drug cheats to evade punishment. Many sports leagues and associations have worked hard to ensure that their biggest stars remain on the field and in the public eye—even if they have been taking PEDs. The MLB is a good example. In the late 1990s and early 2000s, interest in baseball surged, largely based on the achievements of sluggers like Mark McGwire, Barry Bonds, and Sammy Sosa. In 1998 both McGwire and Sosa smashed the single-season home run record of sixty-one, set several decades earlier; three years later Bonds established a new record of seventy-three home runs. While many fans celebrated these achievements, others believed that the new records were not achieved honestly and accused all three men—and others—of using PEDs.

At the time, however, there was no way to be sure. Though baseball had banned steroids in 1991, it did not establish a drug testing program until 2003. Baseball officials blamed the players' union for blocking proposals to test players, but many fans, players, and journalists had a different explanation. "Do you really think Bud [Selig, the commissioner of baseball,] wants to do anything other than make the owners money?"[42] one player asked rhetorically. In this view, baseball authorities were unwilling to do anything that might cast their best players in a bad light. Testing players for drugs would likely result in a slew of positive tests and reveal these new records as fraudulent—turning fans away from the

Russia Unfairly Avoids Discipline

The Russian Olympic team was found to be engaged in systematic doping in 2015. Yet the International Olympic Committee chose not to remove Russian athletes from the 2016 Olympics and has shown no sign of expelling the Russians from the 2018 Winter Games even though Russian athletes may still be doping. Russia's relative wealth (it is the fifth-wealthiest country in the Olympics) and influence on sports (it has the second-highest number of medals) are the most likely explanations for why Russia has not been disciplined. The Russian team has clearly been given preferential treatment.

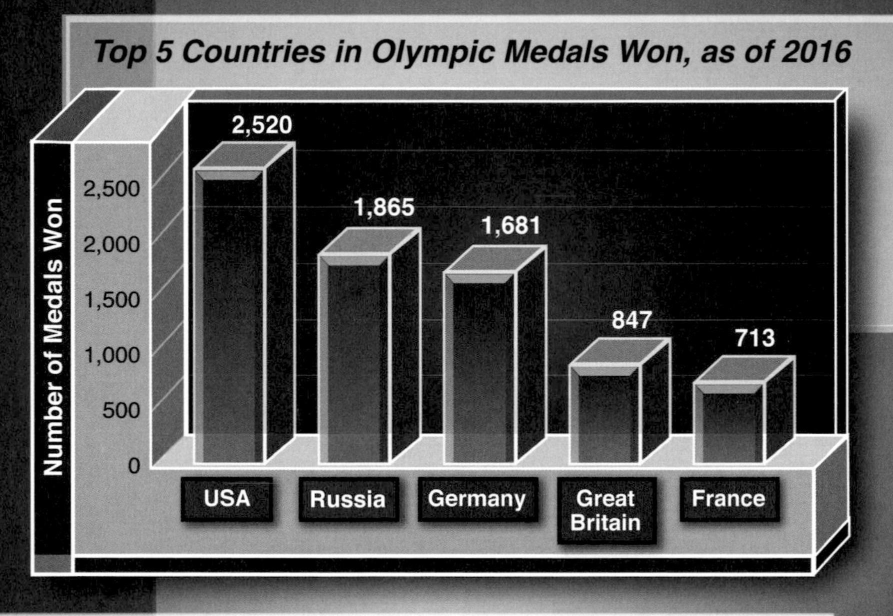

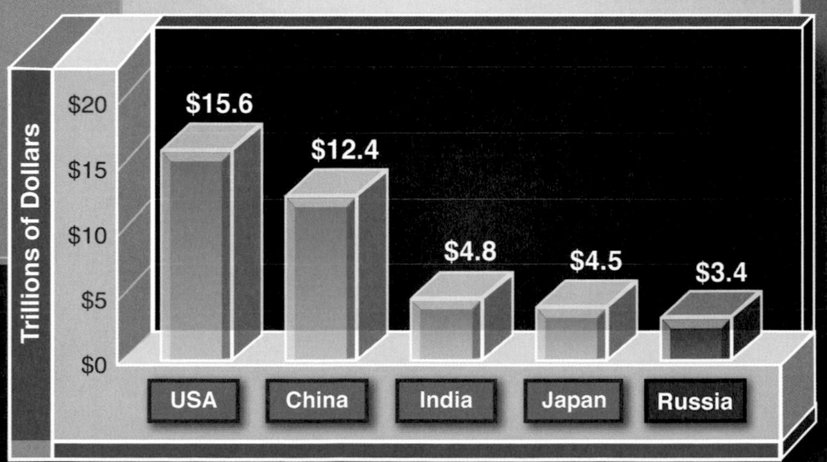

Sources: World Atlas, "Summer Olympic Winners by Total Medals." www.worldatlas.com.
Russia Today, "Russia Breaks into Top 5 World Economies, Displacing Germany." www.rt.com.

sport and cutting into the owners' profits. Thus, while Olympic drug cheats were being tested, caught, and suspended, baseball's best players were off limits.

Baseball was not the only sport to adopt a hands-off approach to drug use in order to protect its star athletes—and its bottom line. Beginning in the early 1990s, cycling was frequently criticized for ignoring massive evidence of doping among its best performers. Matters came to a head when American Lance Armstrong won every running of the long-distance Tour de France from 1999 to 2005. Reports that Armstrong was cheating grew louder with each victory, but Armstrong denied them. The International Cycling Union (UCI) supported Armstrong. Years later, however, it was determined that Armstrong had been cheating all along. Many observers charge that the UCI had known from the beginning but chose not to discipline Armstrong because he had brought new fans and sponsors to the sport. "The UCI was always going to prioritize the image of the sport and the business of the sport over the integrity and the honesty of the sport,"[43] asserts current UCI president Brian Cookson.

"The [International Cycling Union] was always going to prioritize the image of the sport and the business of the sport over the integrity and the honesty of the sport."[43]

—Cycling Union president Brian Cookson

Variations by Sport

Another way in which doping penalties are inconsistent has to do with how different sports and leagues choose to deal with athletes who have doped. In some sports PED use is dealt with harshly; in others it is not. In tennis, for example, a first offense leads to an automatic two-year suspension, and a second results in being permanently barred from competition. In both men's and women's pro basketball, in contrast, athletes who fail drug tests are suspended for just ten games for a first offense; a player must fail four drug tests before incurring a two-year suspension. There are important differences in how many times athletes are tested as well. Most Olympic athletes can expect to be tested multiple times a year, but golfers and hockey players can go a year or more without a single test. Clearly, when standards vary this much, there is no consistency across the sports world.

To make matters worse, some leagues do not have clear guidelines related to drug testing. The National Association for Stock Car Auto Racing, for example, refuses to publicize the list of drugs it tests for. Worse, as a journalist notes, "Suspensions are indefinite and not appealable."[44] The sport thus has extremely broad latitude to punish some athletes more heavily than others, even for identical offenses. College sports are another example. The National Collegiate Athletic Association puts some drug testing in the hands of member schools, some of which take PED use more seriously than others. "Some schools will ban players for a few games on a first offense, while others just let them off with a warning,"[45] writes reporter Kevin Trahan. Trahan cites the University of Alabama and the University of Notre Dame among schools that seldom penalize football players who test positive. As long as variations like these are prevalent, it cannot be said that the penalties for drug testing are uniform or fair. And that represents a serious problem for the legitimacy of drug testing and of sports in general.

Penalties for PED Use Are Generally Consistent and Fair

"With [Maria] Sharapova's outing, tennis officials can claim with some justification that no one is untouchable."

—Michael Steinberger, tennis commentator and journalist

Michael Steinberger, "Maria Sharapova's Drug Scandal May Be Darker than You Think," *Vanity Fair*, March 10, 2016. www.vanityfair.com.

Consider these questions as you read:

1. Can penalties be fair but inconsistent? Can they be consistent but unfair? Why or why not?
2. Which arguments in this section do you think are strongest and which are weakest? Explain.
3. Should penalties be the same across the board for every athlete who breaks the rules, or should sports officials have the ability to adjust punishments according to the specific situation? Why or why not?

Editor's note: The discussion that follows presents common arguments made in support of this perspective, reinforced by facts, quotes, and examples taken from various sources.

Many observers worry that penalties for drug testing in the sports world are unfair and inconsistent. But their focus is misguided. While different sports do have dissimilar guidelines about how to address athletes who test positive, some variation is to be expected. Moreover, the truth is that penalties for PED use have become more and more uniform and unbiased—and are getting more so all the time. Discrepancies in how athletes are treated do exist—and those differences should be minimized going forward. But in the world of sports today, there is little reason to fear that penalties are applied in an arbitrary or unjust way.

Suspensions for Stars

Over the years, observers have identified several reasons for believing that PED penalties are applied inconsistently. One of the most important of these is the concern that leagues and federations are too invested in their star athletes: They do not want to run the risk of suspending their best players. Doing so, after all, would call into question the legitimacy of their sport and might also impact the sport's earnings. In the 1990s and even into the early 2000s, this argument may have had some validity. But today the evidence fails to support it.

One recent example comes from tennis. In 2016 a test revealed that Russian star Maria Sharapova had taken a banned chemical called meldonium, which had only recently been added to the list of banned substances. Sharapova, who had been taking the drug for several years, said that she had simply been unaware that meldonium had been ruled off limits. "I did not do anything intentionally wrong,"[46] she explained. Tennis officials could have chosen not to penalize Sharapova, and such a decision might well have been in the best interest of the sport. Not only is Sharapova one of the top players on the women's tennis tour, she has also done modeling and appeared in countless advertising campaigns, thus putting herself and her sport in the public eye far more than many other athletes. The International Tennis Federation (ITF) had every reason to want to keep Sharapova on the court, and the details of the case made that course of action plausible.

"I commend the commissioner [of baseball] for his leadership on this issue."[48]

—Anti-doping activist Travis Tygart

And yet the ITF did not exonerate Sharapova. Instead, it suspended her for two years (a penalty reduced to fifteen months on appeal). Members of the commission believed Sharapova when she said she had not intended to break the rules, but they chose to ban her regardless. The severity of the sentence was applauded by some who had believed that sports typically had two different sets of standards where drug use was concerned.

Something similar took place in mixed martial arts (MMA), where PED use was once widely ignored. In 2016, soon after hiring former government drug enforcement agent Jeff Novitzky to run its drug testing program, authorities at an MMA event discovered that one of its biggest stars had tested positive for PEDs. Novitzky "said we had no choice," recalls promoter Lorenzo Fertitta. "[The fighter] gets pulled off the card, and we gotta make the best of it."[47] Like tennis, MMA was being consistent even when doing so was not in its interest.

Baseball is another example. Any reluctance the sport once had to implicate its best players is no longer apparent. Indeed, the list of baseball players suspended for PED use since testing began in 2003 includes some of the sport's top performers. Slugger Manny Ramirez, one of just fifteen players to hit more than 550 home runs, was suspended for 50 games in 2009—and 100 games for a second offense in 2011. Outfielder Ryan Braun was named his league's Most Valuable Player in 2011; two years later, he was suspended for nearly half a season for doping. And Alex Rodriguez, one of the greatest players in baseball history, was banned by baseball commissioner Bud Selig for an astonishing 211 games in 2013. "I commend the commissioner for his leadership on this issue,"[48] said anti-doping activist Travis Tygart. Baseball may once have had two different sets of standards, but that was in the past. Like tennis and MMA, baseball today clearly holds all of its players and teams equally accountable.

Greater Consistency

The example of baseball highlights another important point about consistency in penalizing PED users. In the early days of PED use, sports developed wildly different ways of dealing with athletes who doped. Several sports, including baseball, track and field, and weight lifting, ignored PED use for many years. As late as 2005, American lawmaker Henry Waxman was complaining about basketball's "remarkably weak steroids program," while another member of Congress dismissed it as "pathetic."[49] In contrast, the Olympics took a strong stand against drug use early on; Olympic officials carried out several hundred drug tests in 1968 and introduced testing on a full-scale basis four years later.

MLB Shows No Favoritism with PED Suspensions

Major League Baseball has suspended several dozen players for PED use since 2005. Five of them rank among the league's greatest hitters, especially where home runs are concerned: Each has hit over three hundred home runs as of the end of the 2017 season. Three have won Most Valuable Player awards. These are the kinds of players that a sports league would try very hard to keep on the field if there were different standards for different players. Yet MLB chose to suspend them. Clearly punishments for PED use are consistent and fair.

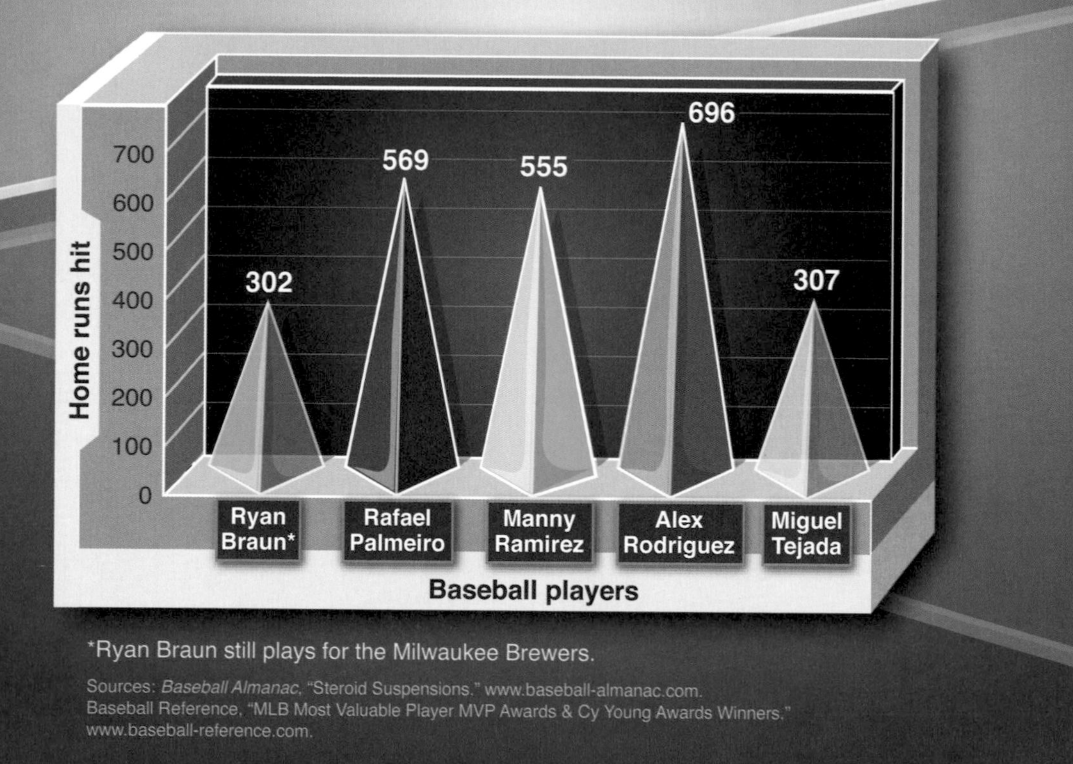

*Ryan Braun still plays for the Milwaukee Brewers.

Sources: *Baseball Almanac*, "Steroid Suspensions." www.baseball-almanac.com.
Baseball Reference, "MLB Most Valuable Player MVP Awards & Cy Young Awards Winners." www.baseball-reference.com.

From these disparate beginnings, though, sports federations have moved rapidly in the direction of consistency. Once again, those who argue that penalties for PED use are inconsistent and unfair are not living in the present. During the 1990s and early 2000s, for example, cycling hardly ever punished drug cheats. But that is no longer the case. Today penalties for cyclists who dope typically range up to two years for a first offense, putting them in line with the penalties for most other sports. In fact, most sports are broadly similar in how they treat drug cheats, and the odds are excellent that through pressure from fans, competitors, and governments, the outliers will soon follow the trend.

Punishments Fitting the Crime

Finally, penalties for doping can be both fair and consistent without insisting that every athlete who fails a doping test receive precisely the same penalty. The American legal system, after all, generally gives judges some latitude in meting out punishment to criminals. Judges may raise or lower penalties based on all sorts of factors, from whether the defendant shows remorse to the degree to which others may have been culpable as well. The same should hold true in the sports world. A wise drug policy will recognize that not all infractions are equal. Judges are not typically expected to be automatons, rigorously applying one-size-fits-all rules regardless of the specifics of a case. The people in charge of penalizing drug cheats should not be robots either.

Indeed, some seemingly inconsistent policies in sports are actually fair and reasonable. The MLB, for example, typically suspends players for eighty games if they test positive for steroids, but the penalty for using stimulants is only twenty-five games. In one sense, that is inconsistent; after all, one penalty is more than three times harsher than the other. In another sense, though, the variation in penalty length is reasonable. Baseball officials disapprove of stimulant use but are far more concerned with steroids. That is a legitimate perspective. Steroids are more effective than stimulants in improving athletic performance and more dangerous to the athletes who take them. Baseball's policy reflects this reality.

"They had their policy, they had their admission and they were not open to negotiation."[50]

—A lawyer representing golfer Scott Stallings

Unfortunately, the call for consistency sometimes causes sports authorities to act in ways that are neither sensible nor fair. The case of golfer

Scott Stallings is an excellent example. In 2015, after taking a hormone that had been prescribed by his doctor, Stallings discovered that the medication was banned by his sport. Stallings immediately reported his mistake to the golf authorities. As with Sharapova, Stallings's use of the drug seemed to be an honest mistake; moreover, Stallings had essentially turned himself in.

But none of that mattered to the commission that handled Stallings's case. "They had their policy," noted Stallings's lawyer, "they had their admission and they were not open to negotiation."[50] The result was a ninety-day suspension, when allowing Stallings to continue competing might well have been the fairer solution. In courtrooms and in sports, punishments should fit the crime, not match some arbitrary definition of consistency.

Source Notes

Overview: Performance-Enhancing Drugs

1. Thomas H. Murray, "The Coercive Power of Drugs in Sports," *Hastings Center Report*, August 1983.
2. Quoted in Ron Hodgetts, "Russian Doping Report Alleges 'Institutional Conspiracy,'" CNN, December 9, 2016. http://edition.cnn.com.
3. Quoted in Associated Press, "Frank Thomas Calls Out Hall of Fame Elects: You Know You 'Cheated,'" *New York Post*, January 29, 2017. http://nypost.com.

Chapter One: Should PED Use by Athletes Be Acceptable?

4. Quoted in *Guardian* (Manchester), "Wada Reveals up to 50% of Drug Tests at 2016 Olympic Games Had to Be Aborted," October 27, 2016. www.theguardian.com.
5. Quoted in Rick Maese, "A Less Glamorous Side of Olympic Life," *Chicago Tribune*, July 16, 2016. www.chicagotribune.com.
6. Quoted in Associated Press, "Ryan Braun Apologizes for PED Use," ESPN, August 23, 2013. www.espn.com.
7. William Saletan, "The Beam in Your Eye," *Slate*, April 18, 2005. www.slate.com.
8. Howard Bryant, *Juicing the Game*. New York: Viking, 2005, p. 146.
9. Quoted in Joe Torre and Tom Verducci, *The Yankee Years*. New York: Doubleday, 2009, pp. 94–95.
10. *Herald Sun* (Melbourne, Australia) editorial staff, "Cycling Must Kick Its Habit," October 23, 2012. www.heraldsun.com.au.
11. World Anti-Doping Agency, *World Anti-Doping Code 2015*. Montreal, QC: World Anti-Doping Agency, 2015, p. 14.
12. Quoted in Andy Layhe, "Ethical Questions on Doping Answered," Bike Pure, January 9, 2010. https://bikepure.org.
13. Quoted in Arthur L. Caplan and Brendan Parent, *The Ethics of Sport*. Oxford: Oxford University Press, 2016, p. 463.

Chapter Two: How Much Do PEDs Actually Improve Performance?

14. Mayo Clinic, "Performance-Enhancing Drugs: Know the Risks," October 15, 2015. www.mayoclinic.org.
15. Quoted in *Men's Health*, "The Amateur's Complete Guide to Blood Doping," August 3, 2017. www.menshealth.co.uk.
16. Quoted in Bryant, *Juicing the Game*, p. 176.
17. Quoted in Dale Tafoya, *Bash Brothers: A Legacy Subpoenaed*. Washington, DC: Potomac, 2008, p. 140.
18. Quoted in Thomas Heath, "McCain Wants USADA to Test Major Sports," *Washington Post*, May 24, 2005. www.washingtonpost.com.
19. Quoted in Mike Puma, "Not the Size of the Dog in the Fight," ESPN Classic. www.espn.com.
20. Lachlan Cartwright and Christian Red, "Yankees Closer Mariano Rivera Says Playing During Steroid Era the Only Thing That Bothers Him About Career," *New York Daily News*, September 27, 2013. www.nydailynews.com.
21. Dave Brown, "Don't Forget That Barry Bonds Was a Hall of Famer Before PED Suspicion," CBS Sports, December 24, 2015. www.cbssports.com.
22. Quoted in *Science 2.0* (blog), "Performance Enhancing Drugs Don't Improve Performance—and Haven't Since 1886," May 4, 2015. www.science20.com.
23. Quoted in Tim Kawakami, "Tony Gwynn Interview from July 2002: 'Sometimes Technique Works Better than a Whole Lot of Other Things,'" *Talking Points* (blog), *San Jose (CA) Mercury News*, June 16, 2014. http://blogs.mercurynews.com.
24. Quoted in Christopher J. Beedie, "Placebo Effects in Competitive Sport: Qualitative Data," *Journal of Sports Science and Medicine*, March 2007. www.ncbi.nlm.nih.gov.
25. Daniel Engber, "The Growth Hormone Myth," *Slate*, March 24, 2007. www.slate.com.
26. Quoted in Natasha Singer, "Does Testosterone Build a Better Athlete?," *New York Times*, August 8, 2010. www.nytimes.com.

27. Quoted in Ian Johnston, "'Performance-Enhancing Drug That Cost Lance Armstrong His Seven Tour de France Titles Doesn't Work, Finds Study." *Independent* (London), June 30, 2017. www.indepen dent.co.uk.

Chapter Three: Does Testing for PED Use Deter Athletes from Doping?

28. Pat Caputo, "Why I Won't Vote for Bonds, Clemens, or Sosa for the Hall of Fame," *New Haven (CT) Register*, January 14, 2012. www .nhregister.com.
29. Quoted in *New Zealand Herald*, "Piers Morgan Calls Armstrong a 'Snivelling, Lying, Cheating Little Wretch,'" January 19, 2013. www .nzherald.co.nz.
30. *New York Daily News*, "A-Roid," February 8, 2009, p. 1.
31. Quoted in Jeff Fletcher, "Angels Notes: Players Believe Starling Marte's Suspension Is a Good Deterrent," *Orange County (CA) Register*, April 18, 2017. www.ocregister.com.
32. Quoted in Mike Dickson, "Maria Sharapova Could Be Expelled from All England Club After Doping Ban," *Daily Mail* (London), June 9, 2016. www.dailymail.co.uk.
33. Quoted in Reuters, "Back in Seoul, Ben Johnson Hopes for a 'New Chance,'" *Toronto Star*, September 24, 2013. www.thestar.com.
34. Quoted in Michael Janofsky, "2 U.S. Track Stars Face 2-Year Ban for Drug Use," *New York Times*, November 6, 1990. www.nytimes.com.
35. Quoted in Sydney Lupkin, "Why Drug Tests Can't Catch Doping Athletes," ABC News, August 8, 2013. http://abcnews.go.com.
36. Quoted in Sean Ingle, "How Cheats Cheat: Why Dopers Have the Edge in Athletics' War on Drugs," *Guardian* (Manchester), August 20, 2015. www.theguardian.com.
37. Quoted in Gretchen Reynolds, "Phys Ed: Will Olympic Athletes Dope If They Know It Might Kill Them?," *Well* (blog), *New York Times*, January 20, 2010. https://well.blogs.nytimes.com.

Chapter Four: Are Penalties for PED Use Inconsistent and Unfair?

38. Quoted in Nathaniel Vinton, "Russia's Track and Field Team Banned from Rio Olympics Due to Doping Conspiracy," *New York Daily News*, June 17, 2016. www.nydailynews.com.
39. Quoted in Sean Ingle, "Anti-Doping Agencies Call on IOC to Ban Russia from 2018 Winter Olympics." *Guardian* (Manchester), September 14, 2017. www.theguardian.com.
40. Quoted in Marissa Payne, "U.S. and 16 Other National Anti-Doping Agencies Call for Banning Russia from 2018 Olympics," *Washington Post*, September 15, 2017. www.washingtonpost.com.
41. Richard Hinds, "Banning Russia from Rio Won't Mark Success in the War on Doping, It Will Just Highlight Previous Failings," *Daily Telegraph* (Sydney, Australia), July 23, 2016. www.dailytelegraph.com.au.
42. Quoted in Bryant, *Juicing the Game*, p. 259.
43. Quoted in Gerry Mey, "Authorities Turned a Blind Eye to Doping in Cycling: UCI Boss," Reuters, March 9, 2015. www.reuters.com.
44. Tania Ganguli, "NASCAR Drug Testing Policy Has Drivers on Edge," *Los Angeles Times*, May 16, 2009. http://articles.latimes.com.
45. Kevin Trahan, "Will Grier's PED Suspension Is Another Example of Why College Athletes Need a Union," Vice Sports, October 14, 2015. https://sports.vice.com.
46. Quoted in Chuck Schilken, "Maria Sharapova Plans to Appeal 'Unfairly Harsh' Two-Year Suspension for Doping," *Los Angeles Times*, June 8, 2016. www.latimes.com.
47. Quoted in Rick Maese, "He Busted Marion Jones and Lance Armstrong; Now Top Steroid Cop Works for UFC," *Washington Post*, May 2, 2016. www.washingtonpost.com.
48. Quoted in Steve Keating, "Praise for Selig and No Sympathy for Drug Cheats," Reuters, August 5, 2013. www.reuters.com.
49. Quoted in Dave Curtis and Richard Lezin Jones, "Lawmakers Pick Apart N.B.A.'s Steroids Policy," *New York Times*, May 20, 2005. http://query.nytimes.com.
50. Quoted in Pete Madden, "Scott Stallings: The Real Story Behind My Tour Drug Suspension," *Golf*, July 21, 2016. www.golf.com.

Performance-Enhancing Drug Facts

Drug Testing

- The first athlete to lose a medal for drug use at the Olympics was Hans-Gunnar Liljenwall, a modern pentathlete, who tested positive for ethanol in 1968.
- While several players have been banned from American sports leagues for use of recreational drugs such as cocaine, baseball pitcher Jenrry Mejía remains the only one permanently suspended for PED use.
- The greatest number of positive test results at the Olympics have been from athletes in track and field, weight lifting, and cycling, in that order.
- The United States and Russia have had the greatest number of positive doping tests at the Olympics.
- The National Collegiate Athletic Association mandates that drug testers visit each Division I college program at least once every year.

Individual Drugs

- Diuretics, which cause people to urinate frequently, are banned by most sports primarily because they can be used to eliminate traces of PEDs from an athlete's system.
- Injectable testosterone was developed in 1935. Its first purpose was to increase aggression in soldiers.
- Some side effects of PEDs include high blood pressure, skin conditions, and heart and liver ailments.
- To be banned as a PED, chemicals must meet at least two of the following qualifications: They are believed to improve performance, they can damage a user's health, and they violate the spirit of sports.

Athletes and Drugs

- Estimates suggest that as many as 30 percent of professional athletes use steroids.
- In 1986 ten NFL players weighed 300 pounds (136 kg). Twenty years later, there were more than three hundred.
- Studies of high school athletes suggest that anywhere from about 2 percent to about 10 percent have taken PEDs.
- One-fourth of former East German athletes surveyed in a 2007 study, each of whom had taken PEDs during their competitive careers, had developed some type of cancer.

Anti-Doping Agencies and Legal Issues

- WADA, or the World Anti-Doping Agency, was founded in 1999.
- The USADA, or United States Anti-Doping Agency, was established in 2000.
- In 2003 US authorities brought charges against a company called the Bay Area Laboratory Co-operative, which had been selling drugs for several years to professional athletes. The company's owner, Victor Conte, was sentenced to a prison term.
- Baseball player Barry Bonds was convicted in 2011 of lying to a grand jury about his PED use.
- Many PEDs, such as anabolic steroids and HGH, are legal in the United States but only by prescription.
- The value of steroids purchased and sold illegally each year, mostly for the use of athletes, is believed to be more than $100 million.
- After the 2005 publication of Jose Canseco's memoir, *Juiced*, a series of hearings about drugs in baseball were held in Congress. Among those who testified were Mark McGwire, Sammy Sosa, and Rafael Palmeiro.

Related Organizations and Websites

Major League Baseball (MLB)
245 Park Ave.
New York, NY 10167
website: www.mlb.com

MLB, which once lagged behind other sports leagues and foundations where drug testing was concerned, now has a much more robust testing program. The league can provide information about the types of drugs it tests for and how the process works.

National Center for Drug Free Sport
2537 Madison Ave.
Kansas City, MO 64108
e-mail: info@drugfreesport.com

This organization manages drug testing programs as well as helps develop drug testing policies throughout the sports world. It also provides educational materials about PEDs and advocates for drug-free competition.

National Institutes of Health (NIH)
9000 Rockville Pike
Bethesda, MD 20892
website: www.nih.gov

The NIH is a major medical research center. Some of its focus is on drugs that are commonly used in sports. The site offers articles and other resources related to PEDs.

Taylor Hooton Foundation
PO Box 2104
Frisco, TX 75034
website: www.taylorhooton.org

This organization advocates against the use of steroids and other PEDs. It provides educational materials to encourage athletes and others to avoid drug use. The foundation focuses its work on teenagers and other young people.

USA Cycling
210 USA Cycling Point, Suite 100
Colorado Springs, CO 80919
website: www.usacycling.org

This is the official site of the American cycling foundation. The site has a number of articles and information sheets regarding health, quite a few of which focus on PEDs.

US Anti-Doping Agency (USADA)
5555 Tech Center Dr., Suite 200
Colorado Springs, CO 80919
website: www.usada.org

The USADA does drug testing for the US Olympic team and other sports organizations. It provides information about the effects of banned PEDs, explains the testing procedures, and offers educational materials in support of the anti-doping position.

United States Olympic Committee
1 Olympic Plaza
Colorado Springs, CO 80909
websites: www.olympic.org/united-states-of-america • www.teamusa.org

This is the official site of the US Olympic team. The site includes many articles, news items, and information sheets of interest to people who follow the Olympics; many of these relate to drug testing and the use of PEDs.

World Anti-Doping Agency (WADA)
800 Victoria Pl., Suite 1700
Montreal, QC, Canada H4Z 1B7
website: www.wada-ama.org

WADA focuses its attention on combating drugs at all levels of sports. The site includes lists of banned substances, information about drug testing procedures, and a link to the *Anti-Doping Code*, which aims for consistency in drug policies across nations and sports.

For Further Research

Books

Arthur L. Caplan and Brendan Parent, *The Ethics of Sport*. Oxford: Oxford University Press, 2016.

Chris Cooper, *Run, Swim, Throw, Cheat: The Science Behind Drugs in Sport*. Oxford: Oxford University Press, 2013.

David Haugen and Susan Musser, eds., *Athletes and Drug Use*. Farmington Hills, MI: Greenhaven, 2013.

Tony Khing, *Performance-Enhancing Drugs in Sports*. Minneapolis: Abdo, 2014.

Juliet Macur, *Cycle of Lies: The Fall of Lance Armstrong*. New York: HarperCollins, 2014.

David R. Mottram and Neil Chester, eds., *Drugs in Sport*. London: Routledge, 2015.

Internet Sources

Daniel Engber, "The Growth Hormone Myth," *Slate*, March 24, 2007. www.slate.com/articles/health_and_science/science/2007/03/the_growth_hormone_myth.html.

Sean Ingle, "Anti-doping Agencies Call on IOC to Ban Russia from 2018 Winter Olympics," *Guardian* (Manchester), September 14, 2017. www.theguardian.com/sport/2017/sep/14/anti-doping-agencies-tell-ioc-ban-russia-2018-winter-olympics.

Sean Ingle, "How Cheats Cheat: Why Dopers Have the Edge in Athletics' War on Drugs," *Guardian* (Manchester), August 20, 2015. www.theguardian.com/sport/2015/aug/20/doping-world-athletics-championships-cheats.

Sydney Lupkin, "Why Drug Tests Can't Catch Doping Athletes," ABC News, August 8, 2013. http://abcnews.go.com/Health/star-athletes-rarely-caught-steroids-drug-tests/story?id=19887238.

Mayo Clinic, "Performance-Enhancing Drugs: Know the Risks," October 15, 2015. www.mayoclinic.org/healthy-lifestyle/fitness/in-depth/performance-enhancing-drugs/art-20046134.

Gerry Mey, "Authorities Turned a Blind Eye to Doping in Cycling: UCI Boss," Reuters, March 9, 2015. www.reuters.com/article/us-cycling-report-cookson/authorities-turned-a-blind-eye-to-doping-in-cycling-uci-boss-idUSKBN0M51OP20150309.

William Saletan, "The Beam in Your Eye." *Slate*, April 18, 2005. www.slate.com/articles/health_and_science/human_nature/2005/04/the_beam_in_your_eye.html.

Michael Steinberger, "Maria Sharapova's Drug Scandal May Be Darker than You Think," *Vanity Fair*, March 10, 2016. www.vanityfair.com/news/2016/03/maria-sharapova-drug-scandal-may-be-darker-than-you-think.

Note: Boldface page numbers indicate illustrations.

About the Author

Stephen Currie has written many books for young adults and children. His works for ReferencePoint Press include *Sharing Posts: The Spread of Fake News*, *Cause & Effect: The Ancient Maya*, and *Forgotten Youth: Undocumented Immigrant Youth*. He has also taught grade levels ranging from kindergarten to college. He lives in New York's Hudson Valley.